THE MAN IN THE YELLOW HAT

American Academy of Religion
Academy Series

edited by
Susan Thistlethwaite

Number 76
THE MAN IN THE YELLOW HAT

by
Dorothy W. Martyn

Dorothy W. Martyn

THE MAN IN THE YELLOW HAT
Theology and Psychoanalysis in Child Therapy

Scholars Press
Atlanta, Georgia

THE MAN IN THE YELLOW HAT
Theology and Psychoanalysis in Child Therapy

by
Dorothy W. Martyn

© 1992
The American Academy of Religion

Library of Congress Cataloging in Publication Data

Martyn, Dorothy W.
    The man in the yellow hat : theology and psychoanalysis in child therapy / Dorothy W. Martyn.
    p. cm.
    Includes bibliographical references.
    ISBN 1-55540-630-0 (alk. paper). — ISBN 1-55540-631-9 (pbk.)
    1. Child analysis. 2. Children—Religious life. 3. Christianity—Psychology. 4. Psychoanalysis and religion. I. Title.
RJ504.2.M37 1991
618.92'8914—dc20   91-29542
                                                                                    CIP

Printed in the United States of America
on acid-free paper

Acknowledgments

I would like to thank Professor Ann Belford Ulanov, who exemplified in her patient guidance of this dissertation the qualities of relationship about which this book purports to speak, and Professor Robert Neale and Donald Bell, M.D., who supported and encouraged its writing. For guidance of the theological chapter, and especially for the theological insights of Karl Barth, I am indebted to Professor Christopher Morse. To Deborah Hample, who enhanced for me the art of Child Therapy, and to Drs. Anthony Burry and Henry Kellerman, I am indebted for the torch of Psychoanalysis. To my husband, J. Louis Martyn, I am grateful for forty years of Biblical and theological riches that have nourished and sustained our shared parental journey.

"And a little child shall lead them."

To all the children who have led me
this book is gratefully dedicated

Contents

Chapter I

THREE THERAPEUTIC JOURNEYS 1

    Amy
    John
    William

Chapter II

INVESTIGATION FROM THE STANDPOINTS
OF TWO MAJOR THEORIES 35

    Freud
    Jung

Chapter III

THE BEGINNING AND DEVELOPMENT OF SYMBOLIC EXPRESSION IN
CHILDHOOD 57

Chapter IV

THE RELATIONAL CONTEXT: CENTRALITY OF OBJECT RELATIONS IN
PERSONALITY FORMATION AND SUBLIMATION 69

      Harry Stack Sullivan
      Melanie Klein
        Centrality of Objects in Personality
        Schema of Emotional Development as Object-Centered
        Symbol Formation and Sublimation in Klein's Theory

Chapter V

THE RELATIONAL CONTEXT: THE HOLDING ENVIRONMENT 91

      D. W. Winnicott
      Ego-Needs
        Mirror-role of Mother and Family
        Ambivalence of Mother and Family

Chapter VI

AMBIVALENCE: SOME IMPLICATIONS FOR AMY, JOHN, AND WILLIAM 109

> Problems Connected With Aggression
> Aggression: William
> Aggression: Amy and John
> Implications for the Parent-Child Relationship of
>   Problems Connected With Aggression
> Narcissism: Parents and Children

Chapter VII

AMBIVALENCE OF FEELING AND PLAY 127

Chapter VIII

A THEOLOGICAL PERSPECTIVE 145

> Karl Barth
>   The Grace and Holiness of God
>   The Mercy and Righteousness of God
>   The Patience and Wisdom of God

Chapter IX

CONCLUSION 167

REFERENCES 177

Chapter I

THREE THERAPEUTIC JOURNEYS

AMY

"My face was invisible. I had to wear a mask. Then they finally found out I had a mask. Then my face came back."

"I was being chased by a monster;..there were roots of a big tree all over the ground, and I kept tripping and falling. I had to keep getting up and running around."

"There was a big dog; it kept jumping and jumping on me."

The child thus described her predicament in her dreams. Why did she find it necessary to wear a mask? What was the monster that chased her, the big animal she had to fend off? What was it that she kept tripping over, and why did she have to stay in motion?

In a course of play therapy, one hour a week over a period of two years, the child laid out these questions for herself and embarked on a journey to find the answers. With her permission, a sketch of that journey in a playroom is presented below.

In the Beginning

Because the child found it necessary to "wear a mask," the adults in her life, her parents and teachers, had a limited view of Amy's inner distress. This engaging eight-year old blonde gave her parents reason for only mild concern. She seemed to be overly conscientious, inordinately anxious to please, and perfectionistic in her standards for herself. Worrying a good deal about what people might think of her, she was quite fearful of making any mistake, had difficulty with attention to detail, and sometimes "blocked" in mathematics. Any sign of conflict in the family sent her running in tears to her room. Easily frustrated, she tended to isolate herself at times and withdrew into books a great deal. Her teacher described her as "wistful and dreamy," and her parents found her more fearful of physical dangers than would seem warranted by her situation in the real world. She seemed overly solicitous about her little sister. Sometimes she wet her bed.

Amy was in many ways a model child. She excelled in school work and delighted her parents and teachers with her thoughtfulness and her exemplary conduct. However, something betrayed the presence of inner difficulty in a way that troubled the benign surface: she developed a nervous habit of clearing her throat frequently, with no apparent cause. When someone called this matter to her attention, she gave up the habit and replaced it with a tic: she began to blink her eyes repeatedly, as though holding back something in that way—some feeling? or perhaps tears?

So Amy appeared to others. And how did she present her situation? In her first session, she brought forth laboriously a picture of a glittering star; at her next visit, the star herself appeared in a dazzling performance. She arrived with a carefully prepared agenda for the session. "I wrote it all down for you," she explained, "but I forgot to bring it. But I know it anyway." Amy then presented me with the most astonishing array of entertainment, which had been carefully prepared: riddles, jokes, stories, some facts she had learned in science class, three dreams, and some other memorized bits that sufficed to fill the hour. She was understandably exhausted at the end of this spectacular display, planned and executed, no doubt, to please this latest adult in her life and to excel in the newly assigned task of psychotherapy.

Reaching tentatively toward the toys the following week, Amy sketched out a battlefield in the sandbox between soldiers in red uniforms and soldiers in blue uniforms. The distribution of power between the two sides—between the reds and the blues—appeared to be a matter of concern. She counted and recounted the numbers of horses and men on both sides and considered thoughtfully whether an advantage of more space for the blue soldiers would help to make up for fewer horses and men. She assigned and reassigned and then assigned again the horses and guns. She mentioned that there were not enough riders for the horses and also began to look around for fences, "to keep out the ones we don't like." She did not reach a satisfactory solution for herself as to the relative power of the opposing forces and seemed to leave that question open. The only hint she gave as to the nature of the conflict was: "The Americans are very angry with the British because of all the bad things the British did."

A first image of her inner situation was thus laid out. It tells us little more than there is a conflict between certain forces, that there is uncertainty about the relative strength of these forces, that there may not be, in her view, adequate control and direction for some of the power, and that there is a necessity for barriers to be erected against unwelcome parties. We are also told that someone is angry at an overlord and that there are "bad things" at the root of the anger.

The paths of a child's imagination lead sooner or later to the "ultimate poetic depth of the space of a house" (Bachelard, p. 6):

> ...All really inhabited space bears the essence of the notion of home....We shall see that the imagination functions in this direction whenever the human being has found the slightest shelter; we shall see the imagination build "walls" of impalpable shadows, comfort itself with the illusion of protection, or, just the contrary, tremble behind thick walls, mistrust the staunchest ramparts. (p. 5)

Amy too came early to the notion of sketching out the setting for her new endeavor in the form of a house. One day, after a long silence, Amy announced that she was going to make a picture. Tentatively, at first, with pencil lines barely visible on the paper, she began to draw some lines and finally announced, "It's going to be a house." Beginning with what amounted to a floor plan, Amy erected, over a period of some weeks, a remarkable paper dwelling, complete with carefully planned and constructed paper furniture in each room.

In the course of the work, Amy expressed a number of concerns, stated pictorially. In rendering a facsimile of a bedroom, with a double bed, she struggled with the problem of inadequate space in the original sketch to accommodate the furniture and, after much erasure and uncertainty, ended by enlarging the walls, quite literally, to alleviate the apparently crowded condition there. In the bathroom, she measured and remeasured the fixtures and, after a week's interval, measured again. She stated emphatically that the toilet was too small and proceeded to make a larger one, after which she again checked its proportions relative to the other furniture in the house. "That's better," she said. The question arises, why did she need a larger facility for elimination? What was it that she needed to get rid of, for which she felt insufficient means of discharge?

She wrestled also with another disproportion. She had begun to devise a playroom in her house, but on second thought decided it should be a workroom, with appropriate appurtenances for study. She assembled a gigantic bookshelf, which towered over the entire house as a colossus. After loading it down with minute paper books, she considered the piece for a while and said, "I like it, but I think it is too tall, don't you?" and proceeded immediately to correct its dimensions relative to the rest of the building.

Further elaborations of the scene introduced other questions. A tree began to grow at one corner of the yard, wrought with paper, crayons, scotch tape, and much perseverance. It seemed that the height and erectness of that tree were of paramount importance to the child, as she worked week after week to remedy its tendency to droop. I reflected to her one day that it seemed important to her that the tree stand up straight and tall. "Yes," she replied, "it has to be strong because I'm trying to put a kid in the swing." What, or who, stood behind this image of a tree that had to be sturdy enough to support the free movement of a child?

Amy's ingenuity in giving vivid symbolic representation to inner concerns gave rise one day to a large red doghouse, far removed from the house proper; in fact, Amy placed the doghouse in the most remote corner of the yard. It seemed that certain inhabitants of her world were not welcome in her main residence and needed to be isolated; that is to say, certain parts of herself needed to be kept separate from the rest of her. Did this structure have some reference, perhaps, to the same theme as the big dog in her dreams, that dog that kept jumping and jumping on her? And did the red color of the house bear some evidence as to what might be sheltered there? Did the red mean red-hot? Did it refer to certain fiery feelings, such as anger, or sexual feelings?

Thus Amy presented in her own way some of her inner concerns through pictorial images. They give us an idea of the kinds of things that were keeping her preoccupied, "wistful and dreamy," a hint or two as to how she was inclined to defend herself against feelings she found to be bad, and some notion of the tight, isolated containment she found necessary to deal with certain parts of herself. Something that was erupting in the form of symptoms—nervous tics, bedwetting, emotional withdrawal—was finding expression in new forms.

Stirrings: Caterpillars, Mice, Worms, and Old-fashioned Ghosts

At last people arrived in the house. A mother paper doll, tall and thin like Amy's own mother found her abode there, along with a little girl with long blond hair, like Amy's. A father doll came too, but Amy changed her mind about him and recast him as a "baby brother," perhaps solving with this revision two problems for herself by condensing into one small, non-threatening sibling the more complex and thorny relationships with father and little sister.

A family now inhabiting the house, other signs of life became evident. Amy came to her session one day accompanied by two live caterpillars in a covered jar. "Their names are Harry and Beggar, and they are going to live in the dog house," she announced. She proceeded, with the help of a stick, to communicate this plan to the caterpillars. These wriggly little creatures did not appear to be enthusiastic about their new residence, and it required repeated efforts of two paper dolls, the mother and the little girl, to corral them into the dog house. In the course of the hour the beasties came at last under satisfactory control of their owners, who, with the help of two pencils, gained considerable expertise in their management. Once the caterpillars were tamed a bit, they were allowed to play on the swing, which now hung triumphantly from the tall paper tree. "Who can manage Harry and Beggar," I asked, "the mother or the little girl?" "They both can," she replied after some thought. These little beasts, allowed to play and swing under the watchful eye of their keepers, represented vital impulses in the child which were relegated to isolation deep within herself, that needed to come forth in her own play sphere. When she reported sadly the following week the untimely death of Harry and Beggar, she added a thought-provoking comment. She sighed and said, "It would have been nice if they could have become butterflies."

The vital stirrings represented by the caterpillars did not depart, however; they found new embodiments. They reappeared one day in a drawing of little mice playing on the grass. Two were playing ball; some were picnicking; one was riding a bike. "There are going to be others," she said. These mice, playing and basking under a bright yellow sun seemed, like the caterpillars, to be giving life to something previously buried deep within her that was now allowed to play a little.

Other images took up this theme. Arriving one day with a troubled look, Amy began her session by saying, "I wanted to show you something, but...look." Unfolding her tightly clasped hand, she displayed a little crumpled heap of green thread. "It was a worm," she explained, "but he wasn't very strong. He only cost ten cents, and I didn't take very good care of him. But I wanted you to see him. He was so nice." I encouraged her to talk about the disappointment and asked her what the worm might have done if he could have survived to come to the playroom. She replied, "Oh, he could sail through the air, and dance, and fly around. He could do all sorts of things. But I knew he wasn't very strong; I should have put him in his little case before I put him in my pocket."

The following week she came happily with another worm, this one only moderately deteriorated, having been better protected. "I'll show you," she said, "what all he can do." Then began a kind of "dance of the worm." With the help of an invisible thread, he flew through the air. Holding her fingers up, Amy demonstrated the worm's agility in going in and out and through her fingers. He danced in and out of the toy stove, under the chair, and frolicked in great freedom around the entire room. Amy's joy in the dancing worm was palpable, and, when this worm met the fate of his predecessor, she was saddened and thoughtful. "I know," she said. "I will make him a coffin." With loving care and much patience, she molded a clay coffin, carefully lining it with black satin and embellishing it with red felt. "The lid must have a handle," she decided; before the little worm in its coffin was interred in a bottom drawer, she had made sure, by gluing a handle on the lid, that some access to what was represented there was indeed secured.

Along with these relatively benign creatures of impulse came others that Amy apparently felt to be less benign. Some "scary and old-fashioned ghosts" came to haunt the playroom for a period, in the form of some handkerchief puppets that Amy designed. They suggested that some very old feelings were beginning to make their appearance in her present-day world. An alligator, with fierce, sharp teeth sounded the theme of aggression in a series of paintings and drawings that followed the arrival of the old-fashioned ghosts. A huge red monster loomed over an entire sheet of drawing paper, with the dubious caption, "I luv you." A snake, bulged out from recently swallowed prey, crept onto the paper and elicited from Amy the comment, "It's a bad snake; it could kill us, you know." A little girl with flaming red cheeks and an enormous mouth that seemed ready to bite nails appeared in another picture. Once loosened, angry and explosive feelings came roaring out in some visual word pictures, illustrating "Bang!" and "Rip!" with brilliant fireworks on display.

Attempts to come to terms with the feelings that found expression in these paintings took varied directions. She experimented with multilayered pictures, such as a red monster sketched out with crayons, covered over heavily with black, with fine stylus lines drawn over the black to let only a hint of the red show through. She designed in both paper and clay a series of monster cartoons, in which she seemed to pursue mastery over these feelings through the time-honored method of humor. Some of these monsters were distinctly female, with long earrings and fancy head-dresses. One was a spider, which was tamed by a lovely hat with colorful flowers, addressing, perhaps, a long-standing fear of spiders mentioned in her history and, no doubt, some figure or force that the spider represented.

Some pictures appeared that took the tack of the opposite pole from the bad feelings. Dolphins, "which are friendly and let you ride on them sometimes," inhabited a sunny, pleasant harbor in one drawing. However, in a succeeding version, the dolphin found himself jumping through red hoops, as though it might be a good idea to put some restraint on this playful fellow. Amy had not made final peace with her aggressive feelings; as one of her miniature figures put it one day, "I still feel like an Indian."

The Search for Containment

When a child, in our society, says that she "still feels like an Indian," she may be saying that she still feels troubled with aggressive impulses. What can be done about such feelings? Perhaps a tighter container than a doghouse, perhaps a jail would serve the purpose? Some bad robbers entered the scene one day, only to find themselves immediately taken captive in a fight with some Lego policemen, who hauled the culprits off to a jail of wooden blocks. Amy seemed dissatisfied with this solution, however, and, after some thought, began to build a "deeper place," as she put it, "where bad guys go when they are *really* bad." This deeper place was concretely established by a revised architecture: more blocks were called into service, and a two-level jail replaced the one-level kind. The offenders "who were really bad" could now be assigned to the more secure facility of the lower floor. Was Amy suggesting an unconscious by this architecture, an unconscious where the "really bad" could be housed?

Further action on the security front took place in this same session by means of the small cars. A speeding vehicle encountered a police car, and both vehicles disappeared under the sand. "I like it better," she said simply, "covered up with sand." Then a bus went out of control, literally tearing around the sandbox, raising dust and leaving a scene of destruction in its path. On inquiry, Amy revealed that "the bus was very angry and had to be stopped." With the help of the police car and a tow truck, she hauled the bus into a parking place and used some small rocks to anchor the wheels. She seemed satisfied with this solution of control over unruly forces, indicating that the rocks should certainly "hold him," since the wheels could now not move at all.

From one perspective, Amy's entire journey in the playroom could be viewed as a search for appropriate containment of her impulse life, some means of housing vital energies without losing contact with them. She had begun depicting this search by her image of the doghouse, continued it by means of the jail, as well as the coffin for the little worm, and carried it further with a sequence of play with houses made of cards. She began to experiment one day with the playing cards, trying one way and another to build four-walled structures with them. "They are for the animals," she said. "Each animal is going to have its own house." The booths she made proved to be quite precarious, however, and, in addition, Amy objected to the closed-off effect of the booths. Booths with one side left open, as a suggestion of a door, proved too fragile for entrance and egress of the animals, and, at the end of a discouraging hour spent in attempts to fortify the card structures, the house of cards came tumbling down. "Well," she sighed, "it doesn't matter. Next time I'm going to build a stronger house."

The next week, the stronger house began to take shape, this time made with wooden blocks. She assessed each animal as to size and provided each with a separate booth. "They are going to have doors this time, because I want to be able to reach them; I want to play with them, you see."

Indeed, Amy had some plans for these animals, plans which required accessibility. The cow, for example, came out of her house one day, walked up to the fence that surrounded the animal compound and surveyed the land beyond the enclosure. "The cow," said Amy, "likes to pretend she can't get out. You see, she used to be in captivity, and, while she likes being more free, sometimes she likes to remember what it was like when she was in captivity." The tiger had the duty of "watching for wild things," and the troublesome hippopotamus, who could not control his bicycle, had to be securely bound to his vehicle with rubber bands. Amy's statements about these animals continued the theme of freedom: "These animals," she said, "are very lucky. They can do lots of things—not like the animals that are in captivity."

The motif of containment for vital impulses in forms that would allow some freedom kept finding new expression. One day, while Amy was telling me about some interesting things she was making at school in connection with an Indian project, her hands took up some string, and she began idly to work with it. Soon she began to weave something out of the string, which turned out to be a sort of container. "It could hold something, I think," she said, as she began looking around the room for "something it could hold." The following session, she made a little paper box, made a sign reading "Amy," and put the sign in the box. Later on, she picked up the box, mused about it and said, "It's too small; we need a bigger one." Cleverly manipulating paper, scissors, and tape, she produced a larger version and attached a sign that read, "The Big Box."

The Big Box stayed on the table, and each week Amy put things inside it. She made a tiny jack-in-the-box, considered it, and said, "It doesn't work very well." She then made another, a more tightly constructed jack-in-the-box, pronounced it good, and placed it inside the Big Box. A small stuffed bird accompanied Amy to her session one day, and he too went into the box. However, Amy looked troubled as she put the bird in the box and said, "I'm going to do something I've been thinking about for a long time." She took the bird from the Big Box and moved to a table where she liked to work with clay. She began to construct something from the clay after carefully measuring the bird with her hand. She began by saying, "You know, I really don't know what this is going to be." However, by the end of two sessions of tenacious effort, she had produced, to her moderate satisfaction, a kind of open, grill-work structure that she announced was a "cage" for the bird.

When Amy arrived the following week to find that the cage had collapsed, she was discouraged but not defeated. "I know what I will do," she said, and, within the hour, she had made a handsomely construed and sturdy birdbath, firmly reinforced by some wooden sticks. She retrieved the bird from the Big Box and, with an air of triumph, settled it snugly into its new abode, apparently quite pleased with her new creation. She had designed a living space for the bird—and the life force within herself represented by the bird—that offered some distinct advantages to both: the birdbath had a sturdy base; it was open to the air, providing the quality of freedom; and it had the added accommodation of life-giving water. Had the vital stirrings that we first saw in the wriggly caterpillars, the dancing worm, and the animals "out of captivity" now found some acceptable containment, less radical than total enclosure and open to the freedom of sky and breeze?

Changes: Enlarged Boundaries

A large, smiling snail crawled out onto Amy's drawing paper one day, and it kept reappearing in picture after picture. What might the spiraling chambers of this creature be representing to the child? Amy did not share with me her own thoughts. My own silent associations recalled a poem memorized in childhood, about a chambered nautilus:

> Build thee more stately mansions, O my soul,
> As the swift seasons roll,
> Leave thy low-vaulted past...

And, indeed, Amy began to confirm that she was sounding the motif of growth and enlarged boundaries. She brought with her one day a doll with a retinue of belongings: a suitcase, clothing for all occasions, a dog with two puppies, a mama horse and a baby horse, various pieces of toy furniture, and a hatbox stuffed with jewelry. "She's getting ready to move," she announced, "because her old house is too small and too crowded." Matter of factly she began construction on a new edifice with the building blocks, making numerous modifications and enlargements as the enterprise proceeded. When she was satisfied as to the adequacy of the new house, she started to construct a station wagon, which grew, and grew, and grew until she was sure it would "hold all the girl's things for moving." Then came the big moment. She piled all the possessions of the doll onto the station wagon and, with the excitement appropriate to such an important event, maneuvered the entire paraphernalia into the garage of the new house. Soon afterwards, the doll was successfully installed in the new dwelling, complete with a warm hearth provided by a clay fireplace and home-baked bread shaped carefully from the play dough.

For many months Amy expressed through the life of the doll certain changes she felt to be taking place within herself. She provided for all the needs of her heroine, who had found a yet stronger dwelling within a drawer, less subject to the exigencies of building blocks. She brought, first of all, a companion doll—"to be her friend"—and gave thought to the dolls' requirements. She gave them food for sumptuous dining; she took them frequently to the beach for pleasure outings; she arranged and rearranged their furniture, "in order to have more space." They were provided by their creator with paper books, made especially for them, and each week they were given a new book, in hand, to enjoy during her absence. One day, Amy changed her mind about leaving the girls with books in their hands: "I think they should do something else," she said. "After all, they can't read all the time. I'm going to let them play with the animals instead." The child was clearly making reference to her own tendency to withdraw into books as a way of avoiding the risks of a fuller life; she was beginning to consider other options.

As the weeks passed, Amy's parents and teachers began to notice changes. The nervous tic—the involuntary, repetitive blinking of her eyes—disappeared. Reports from school revealed a happier, friendlier little girl, who no longer had spells of forgetting what she had wanted to say, and the problems in mathematics were a thing of the past. Amy was able to express her feelings more openly; she could get angry when the occasion called for it, and she did not seem so fearful of physical dangers.

Amy expressed the alterations she sensed to be going on in herself by addressing, from time to time, her fantasy in regard to a rendition she had made earlier of her dog, Spot. She had used gray clay for the body of the dog and had superimposed white spots. She had been critical of the appearance of the dog when she made him, and had said, "He sure is fat, and he's kind of ugly." Nevertheless, she had decided to keep the dog; she placed him in a drawer, which over the months of her work became a museum of all her pieces in clay. From time to time, she removed the dog and mused about him, pondering his appearance, but she did not reveal her thought. Many months later, she removed the dog, looked at him, and said, "You know, I'm not sure this is the way Spot really is. I'm not sure whether he is black with white spots or white with black spots. Sometimes he looks one way, and sometimes he looks the other way. If you look at him from one direction, maybe he's black with white spots, and, from the other direction, he's white with black spots. Hmm." Later still, she considered the question once more and said, "You know, I'm pretty sure Spot is white with black spots, and not black with white spots." She then proceeded to make a new version of the dog, reversing the proportion of black to white, then considering the two models, side by side, announced: "I like the new one better." This revision tells us something about how Amy felt about herself at the beginning of the work and how she changed this perception. Something shady, "fat," and "ugly" had yielded to something more acceptable in her mind's eye; figure and ground had been reversed in her self image.

At this writing, Amy still comes to the playroom, but her journey is nearly ended. She told her mother one day, "I think when I have finished fifth grade, I will not be coming here anymore." It is clear to her, to her parents, and to me that her play therapy, as a particular kind of enlargement of her boundaries, has nearly reached completion. She no longer feels it consistently necessary to wear a mask. The monster that kept chasing her—the bad feelings within, which had kept her on such a treadmill of attempted perfection—has been partially tamed and less rigidly contained. The deeply buried roots, which kept tripping her up—the unconscious obstacles to her growth—have been uncovered sufficiently by her own creative search to loosen their hold on her. The "big dog," which kept jumping and jumping on her turned out not to be so gigantic after all. Her own aggressive feelings, as represented by her dog, Spot, have taken their place in that manageable combination of good and bad with which all of us human beings must learn to live. A metamorphosis has somehow taken place.

JOHN

"He's always going forward, but his car is always left behind," said the child, explaining the plight of the driver of a toy car that seemed to keep getting stuck.

John was speaking, of course, only ostensibly about the toys; he was speaking about himself. He was describing rather accurately his own difficulty in the world beyond the playroom, namely that he was always finding himself separated from his power and feeling himself to be stuck.

His parents, at their first visit, recounted an incident from the previous school day. In a gym meet at school, John had started to take part in a rope-climbing contest. He began competently enough, but after two or three moments gave up, slid down the rope, and walked sadly off the gym floor. On a field day the previous Spring, a similar thing had happened. He was running a race. The child was a strong runner, and toward the end of the race, he found himself out ahead, near the finish line. To the bewilderment and disappointment of his parents, he suddenly dropped back, lost ground to the next runner, and relinquished all chance of winning. After the race, he went off by himself and did not want to talk about it.

In school, John was also not winning. He was dropping back behind his classmates in a manner reminiscent of the race. Though clearly intelligent, he was not inclined toward academic achievement.

He forgot his homework, rarely finished an assignment, and his parents and teachers found it necessary to remind him constantly to attend to his responsibilities. His teacher spoke of him as "extraordinarily sad and withdrawn," tense, and on the edge of what was happening at school. John was not joining in with the other nine-year-olds; he was a "dreamer," who wanted to draw pictures all day long.

In an early session, John decided to draw a picture for me and selected a toy rescue van as an object to copy. With singularly tight and painstaking effort, countless erasures, and a line so light it could scarcely be seen, he sketched a microscopic likeness of a little man, submerged in water and tied by a rope to a boat. Some rescue vehicles were approaching. "This is going to be very small," said John, "so if I mess up, you won't notice it." In the following session, in the course of his play, John called in a rescue unit to save a little figure "who had nearly drowned for lack of oxygen."

A few sessions readily provided several questions: Why did this able young fellow feel so separated from his power? What was preventing him from climbing to the top of the rope ladder, from winning a race, from using his intellectual gifts in school? What was he drowning in, and what did he mean by "lack of oxygen"? Let us see what he tells us in his play.

Of Soldiers, Swords, and Battle Dress

"What's this? There's something wrong here," said John, in his very first hour in the playroom, as he surveyed a group of toy soldiers on a table. Out of the dozens of toys around the room, his eye had selected one item as noteworthy: one of the horsemen had a small irregularity on the arm, a defect in the molding or decorating of that particular piece. John picked up the soldier and mused aloud, "I wonder how he got that way—whether there was something wrong in the way this guy was made, or whether his sleeve is tearing off." As he began to play with the soldiers, he kept coming back to the question he had raised, and, in the course of battle, one horseman called out to this cavalryman, "What's happened to you? Why is your coat falling off?" In the same hour, he called attention to the better protection supplied to the soldiers of the French army, who wore trousers, as opposed to the English, who wore kilts. He also made special note of some little figures in a rescue unit, pointing out to me that the flippers for swimming were "a little small for the man's foot."

Thus John sounded the opening bars of a theme he was to develop and work out in his play in the ensuing weeks and months, that is, a concern for bodily integrity and a preoccupation with adequacy of size. Whenever he played with the soldiers, he was sensitive to the relative sizes of their swords and the comparative appearance of their uniforms. One day he mused out loud that it would be nice if two of the soldiers could exchange swords: "One is short and stubby and there is nothing special about it." Finding that the swords were removable, he did indeed exchange them. Then he reflected that the soldier with the smaller sword had better protection in the form of a shield. "See, if someone hit your hand with a sword, the shield would help protect it. Also this soldier has a better belt, which could not come untied and lose all the attached equipment."

The soldier with the strange arm was taken up from time to time, and his plight was considered. John could not make up his mind about the cause of the irregularity. "We never did decide," he said, "what is wrong with this soldier—whether it was a mistake, or just a fancy jacket, or whether the sleeve got torn in a battle." He excluded this soldier from the army that was lining up for a siege, "because," he said, "he looks so weird; there's something weird about him." Instead, he decided to call into battle a "masterswordsman." "This masterswordsman has many swords. He carries five, and he also has a special one, a gold one, which he does not take out....He might take it out, if he was about to lose, but that hasn't happened yet." The masterswordsman takes the day quite easily, as his opponent, "who has no sword at all," is at a further disadvantage; "He doesn't get killed, but he faints. He faints so often, I don't know why they put him in, but they did."

The hazards of military life frequently included elements beyond insufficient weaponry and courage, namely the certain risks involved in pursuit of power. One Indian warrior was entirely swallowed up in a trap he had inadvertently slipped into when he was trying to take a fort. The moral was clear: as John stated it, "This is what can happen to you if you want to be first." A second version of that moral was sounded when a warrior met death in battle and was duly buried with a gravestone inscribed, "Too fast and too good."

The Power of Wheels

In our culture, there is perhaps no more common symbol for power than the car. Early in John's work, the issue of power via the mighty wheel came to the fore. Playing with a Lego set one day, he constructed a motorcycle and decided it should have three wheels, instead of two, "like they have in England." He added the third wheel, but was still dissatisfied. "I think a car is better than a motorcycle," he said, and he proceeded to build a car. He then compared the car with the motorcycle and explained to me the various advantages of the four-wheeled vehicle over the three-wheeled one. He also demonstrated for me how the car was steadier and could manage the bump on the table better. "The motorcycle," he said, "is definitely less steady on the bumps." In addition to the number of wheels, the size of the wheels was an important consideration. "I used to think," he said, "that there were just two sizes of wheels, big wheels and little wheels, but later I found out there were three sizes." "You see," he showed me, "these middle-sized wheels are the best size." I wondered what John was referring to with these thoughts. Would the big wheels have the same danger as "too fast and too good," and the small wheels the disadvantage of inadequate power to manage the bumps? Were big wheels Father's wheels? John did not say more about it, but we can be certain he was addressing an issue of central concern to him, namely his own power relative to that of significant others in his life.

Another model of the car appeared a few months later, this time with all the advantages of a racing car. This racing car was "super-powered," and John kept adding more and more motors to it, until it had nine. He explained to me that it had so much power that there was no one to race with, except "Blue Flame, who has jets." The figure behind "Blue Flame" was not identified, but one likely candidate might be an accomplished older brother, who seemed to excel at everything he attempted. That John had some oppressive feelings toward this rival might have been suggested by a further addition to his nine-motored racing car. "All the motors have to have exhausts," he said, and proceeded with this refinement. John, like Amy, felt the need of more ample means of discharge of noxious substances, that is, unwelcome feelings. John also equipped his vehicle with an unusual accessory: a special "mud wheel," which he explained would keep his car from getting stuck. Since "getting stuck in the mud" was a major theme of John's play, it is understandable that a mud wheel on his racing car would be a distinct advantage on the road.

Of Mud and Quicksand

The toy soldiers John put into battle in his first session seemed to have a lot of trouble finding solid footing. The child remarked that the soldiers kept falling over; he suggested that the reason might be muddy battlefields. "It is nearly all mud," he said, and by using clay and play dough, he was able to depict a thoroughly muddy terrain for the battle. From week to week, the soldiers and the horsemen and the army vehicles and the cars found themselves stuck in the mud. That soldier "who fainted so often that I don't know why they put him in" not only got stuck in the mud, but on more than one occasion found himself buried up to his head in quicksand and was barely rescued in time to save his life. John remarked that the little fellow didn't like the feeling of mud and quicksand, but he continued for weeks to get bogged down in it.

In one mucky scene, John said of his hero: "For two days, he was just a blob of mud; he couldn't even move at first. If he had stayed like that any longer, he would have hardened, and he would have been just a statue." A narrow escape followed when the soldier fell off a transport truck "in very slushy ground" and found himself once more "almost entirely covered up with mud." Fortunately there was "a bubble in the sand that enabled him to breathe." "The others," John said, "were very glad he found that hole, so that he could live a little longer." Sometimes, John would undertake to clean up the soldiers' boots and pick the mud off their uniforms, as though that action itself had some efficacy for his own situation. One soldier, who had become so encased in mud that he just could not be cleaned up was discarded from the battle.

A variation on the theme of feeling stuck in mud was dramatized in a sandbox, where cars and their drivers kept getting buried in the sand and where all human efforts seemed impeded by the instability of ground. In the first scene John sketched in the sandbox, some people were trying to build a fountain. "They tried and tried, but the sand was just too soft." Then they tried to build a monument, and they managed to get a few stones put together, but, alas, the whole operation gave way, and the entire work party was buried under the sand. "It turned out," he said, "to be more like a graveyard,...where it was necessary for him to scratch himself out a little room." The hero, to whom the "him" referred, found it necessary to wear diver's goggles and an oxygen tank to survive at all under all that sand, "because it was so thick." John, speaking through his miniature representative, was clearly asking for help for himself when he called into the scene a helicopter, "a strong rescuer to come and dig way down underneath" to pull that little fellow out of the grim scene of sand interment.

Of New Highways

While these frequent scenes of mud and sand revealed John's feelings of powerlessness, of being stuck, he was from the first sounding another theme, one of hope and new directions. Two months after he had begun his therapeutic work, John was showing me how a little man could get rescued from repeated falls into the mud by a "nature exploring team," which had been discovered by the "captain." This nature exploring team brought in two helicopters and life boats and oxygen tanks and undertook a series of rescue efforts that freed the repetitively stranded hero of John's stories. I wonder whether John was referring, with the two helicopters, to the fact that his parents were also coming for sessions once a week and whether he sensed the additional power for the rescue operation to lie in this doubling of vehicles.

"He has found a better place to hold on," John announced one day, in the course of pulling his little man out of a sand trap with the help of a string tied to a helicopter. Furthermore, when some of the men "were stuck out on a desert," they didn't give in at all to despair and helplessness. "They are going to look for gas," he explained, "and they are going to find oil out there too." The captain of this party loaded himself down with equipment for this search: he carefully strapped on a power-pack, an oxygen tank, a first-aid kit, and even "when he ran out of power," he did not give up, but started on a second journey "to look for gas and a more level road." Though adversities multiplied, and "it was cold on the desert at night and hot in the daytime," the captain persevered until he found a rescue boat that had gasoline in it.

Thus encouraged, he started to "build new roads," which, however, he did not find to be an easy task. When he tried to make a new road, he found that he kept "knocking sand on the others," and the dirt kept coming back every day, "so that the highway became so messed up, you could hardly tell it was a highway." Apparently there was a lot of fall-out involved in new road building that affected relationships, and, in addition, old materials kept reappearing and getting in the way of the new.

The builder wanted to make a "super highway," but "he just couldn't seem to manage it." The scene was "just a big mess," with cars running amuck everywhere, careening recklessly around, running into each other, landing in a heap. To what did this scene of chaos refer? Was it his external world or his interior world that he felt to be in chaos, or was it both? In any case, John was feeling inadequate order in his life for running his car, and there was a great deal of collision with other vehicles. He wanted a new road and was trying hard to find it.

One of the difficulties in building the new road was referred to several times: "the sand was too soft." Clearly the child's intense interest in carving out for himself a "more level road" that would enable him to avoid getting stuck so often kept hitting a construction problem: the new building material did not harden to great strength overnight. John sensed that some new building was going on within, but he was quite realistically aware, deep inside, that "the sand was still soft," and that it was not going to provide him a hard and dependable surface for travel without repeated effort.

A frequent hazard that impeded the progress of the new road building was a "water trap," which the hero narrowly escaped. Indeed, a fence fell into the water trap, creating a very risky situation, since the fence was to have prevented the cars from falling into the water. Did John perhaps feel that his own defenses were unreliable and subject to slipping? One his cars nearly fell into the trap, but John managed to rescue it just before it disappeared beneath the surface.

Soldiers and vehicles falling into and nearly drowning in "big lakes" and rivers recalled John's first picture of the faint little man who was submerged in water and tied by a rope to a boat. Apparently something pictorially represented by water was a threat to the child's sense of power, a "dread and desire," (to draw upon Freud's formulation of ambivalence of feeling), of being engulfed by something that would keep him passive and helpless, hindering his independent movement. In order to build a new road for himself, John clearly had to confront and master this formidable danger of engulfment by some force—both life-giving and treacherous—that must have wielded some powerful attraction, as well as risk. Otherwise, why would those soldiers and cars be forever finding themselves so close to the water?

Of Robbery and Retribution

John dramatized, over and over, one theme that is intriguing to ponder. An example would be the following story:

The scene was a fort, made of blocks, a very heavily defended and constantly guarded fort, where "gold was kept." A robber came in a truck, faked a delivery, gassed the guard at the entrance, and got away with the gold. The robber was pursued by the authorities and duly imprisoned, but the robber escaped from the prison and repeated the crime, this time with a stronger truck. Central to the story was a "secret passage-way," in which the robber hid. While the policemen searched and searched for the culprit, they had a great deal of trouble capturing this elusive robber.

Other versions of this story emphasized the extreme dangers to which the robber was exposed: bombs would go off in the secret passageways, or an earthquake might destroy the entire scene, and the hero would narrowly escape death. In one version, the gold was in a bag that belonged to a town marshal, and an Indian got away with the gold. The marshall "got shot by mistake....No, I guess he'd better not get killed; let's just say he got knocked out....No, I think he'd better be killed." At that point, however, there was a disjuncture in the story: suddenly John decided to stop playing the game and decided to build a police car instead. A strong urge for the intervention of an authority apparently was felt with enough force to interrupt the story before it was finished. Some anxiety had changed the course of John's play, and it had something to do with theft and murder and an urgent need of a controlling figure.

Such an interruption leads to the question, what is there about the theme of robbery and retribution that gives this motif its perennial impact? If John Steinbeck was correct in his remark that "a story lives when it tells a man about himself," it must be that there lies deep within each of us some primordial fantasy of a crime of robbery against some powerful authority.

For example, a recent motion picture has stolen the heart of the American public. The film is a stirring account of a risky, perseverant, and nearly successful robbery of gold from a heavily guarded moving train. The excited involvement of the audience is palpably on the side of the robber. When the robber is at the last moment apprehended for his crime, only to have his punishment humorously brought into question by the possibility of a fantastic escape, the observers find themselves rejoicing hilariously with the admiring crowd in the film itself: the culprit may, after all, "get away with it."

Is there some remote part of us which feels a horrible kinship with Macbeth, who arranged for the murder of the rightful king in order to usurp his place? Is it that kinship that explains the moral relief that is expressed when Macbeth is reduced?

> Now does he feel his title hang loose about him,
> like a giant's robe upon a dwarfish thief.

Apparently there is something eternally potent for the human psyche in the story of filial thievery. Freud was so convinced of some ever renewed guilt in human experience around this theme that he hypothesized an actual pre-historic patricide by a horde of jealous sons, a deed repressed and ever recurrent in the Oedipal guilt reactivated in each generation. The necessity to deal with that guilt he saw as the genesis of religion, morals, and human government (Freud, 1913b). In both Hebrew and Christian scripture, a primal crime against God the Father is central to the human story.

However one conceives of the realities behind the perpetual human resonance with stories of filial robberies, with attendant risks and ensuing punishments, it was clear in the odyssey of the child John that the theme was a powerful one for him. Early and late in his journey he laid out and wrestled with the problem of criminal offense against authority and the threat of retribution. Once a creature named "Big Foot," who was the reigning power over a mountain fort, was challenged by a young hero, who was trying to climb the mountain, and was "looking for a place to hold on." Big Foot pushed the young hopeful off the mountain, and a terrible struggle between the two ensued. The hero managed to gas Big Foot and put him out of the picture for a while, but "Big Foot still had a lot of power," and in the end regained his rightful place in the mountain, "where he belonged," and the author of the story sighed in relief, saying, "Whew, I'm glad that's over."

Most often the struggle was depicted as one between a captain and some lesser figure. It was an army captain who intimidated the young soldier who "fainted so often," and it was a captain who was so amply supplied with swords that he carried five and had the special one, the gold one, that he did not take out. A "non-officer," being pursued by this masterswordsman, met a sad fate: "He just kept sinking in the boat and nearly drowned. But they managed to pull him out just in time, and he was saved." The struggle between these two figures had begun over access to "a secret place," reminiscent of the secret tunnel of the robbery scenes, "where boats could come." "But the other boats don't know it is there; they probably think it is just solid rock there." John also suggested that the entire scene was "very old." "When the battle took place, this scene was already two hundred years old." Whatever the focus of the dangerous contest between a captain and a "non-officer" over a mysterious refuge, the feelings about it were old feelings—that is, they had been there a long, long time.

In another version of a power struggle, the prize for the winning contestant was to be control over a mountain hideout with many secret doors. The soldiers "who had the least power" succeeded in taking over the mountain at one point by tricking their overlords, but they did it at great risk to their lives. The overlords came after them; the escape routes "got narrower and narrower;" furthermore, the swords of the powerful enemy were planted in the sand in such a way that the insurgents were in imminent danger of death by falling on them. John kept repeating, "Nobody got hurt, so it was all right," as though to reassure himself in some way.

In a different version, an outlaw cavalryman who "caused a lot of trouble," and "who couldn't be trusted," was repeatedly imprisoned behind a tall fence. When the fence could not contain him, a stronger fence was provided; when the stronger fence also proved inadequate, the culprit was placed in a deep pit, "until he learned not to rob anymore."

Of Open Competition

In time, John brought openly into the playroom his fear of competition and faced the fear. After months of sketching out veiled dramas of competitive struggles, he suddenly took another tack. Looking around the room at the beginning of an hour, his eye fell on a shelf of board games, and he invited me to a game of Monopoly. While Monopoly ad infinitum seemed to me to be an endless detour on an otherwise exciting journey, the game culminated in significant issue.

One day, John found that he had managed to accumulate virtually all of the money and property and, in fact, sufficient power to vanquish his opponent utterly. Suddenly, he began to dawdle, fool around, find distractions. He began to offer to lend me money without interest and to say, "Skip it," when I landed on his property and owed him rent. He began to seem bored with the entire enterprise. "John," I said emphatically, "you do not want to win." He conceded my point, and then we explored the question of when he had felt that way before. He recalled the field-day race when he had been winning and deliberately dropped back. He wasn't sure why he had done that dropping back; maybe it was because it might be a good thing for that other fellow to have a chance to win. He was not sure about who might be angry at him if he won sometimes. We left that question open, and John had to go through many more Monopoly games in order to work through, in this safe place, his fear of winning over a competitor. In time, he was able to appropriate my communication that it is all right for boys to grow up and be even better than their fathers at what they do. He learned to enjoy winning a game, even when the adversary was his older brother or father; he took the new freedom to win to the outside world.

John practiced winning in the playroom for many months. Then he tried something more daring: He chose to compete for—and won—a role in a professional production of the opera, *The Magic Flute*. That this opera is a story about a hero's overcoming all possible obstacles to victory, through trials of fire and water and all manner of tribulations is perhaps a coincidence; however, it is striking that the story begins with the hero's overcoming a danger of being swallowed up by a dragon and culminates in the triumphant achievement of his highest ends. John played the role of one of the three Spirits in the opera who help to guide the hero and heroine through their trials. He struck the same motif—of a spirit—in a drawing that he showed me shortly before he decided that he no longer needed the shelter of play therapy. The drawing, which depicts a large horned spirit hovering over a house, bears the caption, "This is a spirit coming to this house." Whatever else is being illustrated by this drawing, the house has reference to himself, and the horned spirit makes a transparent allusion to a sense of forceful strength that the child is beginning to claim.

On Joining the Team

A few weeks before his scheduled departure from the playroom, John left the competitive games and returned to the toy figures who had struggled their way through all those adventures, those defeats and triumphs that so closely paralleled his own. A last drama was sketched out. A young hero engaged once more in a robbery, and tried to make off with hidden treasure, as before. But this time, the story had a different ending. The "bad one" was apprehended and "got his mind changed." "Someone convinced him," said John, "that if he joined the team, he could be a leader."

Thus John found an ancient solution to an ancient dilemma having to do with sons and fathers (and, of course, with daughters and mothers): if you cannot defeat them, join them. The fear of competition, which seemed throughout John's journey to have some reference to his father—a reference screened, as it frequently is, through the older brother—had been alleviated. He had worked his way through to a degree of identification with the father's power and was ready to relinquish part of the competitive struggle with him.

In the world beyond the playroom, John's gains were modest but decisive. He could now go out and compete with other boys without the crippling fear of being stronger than his father and the attendant guilt about wanting to displace him. He could go on to the top of that rope ladder now and could allow himself to win a race. While there were many tasks yet to be accomplished in the long adventure of growing up, he had killed one giant dragon in his path: he was no longer compelled to lose.

WILLIAM

"Hitting people in the face, that's what I'm good at," said this seven-year-old belligerently. And hit people in the face, he did. Because he could not abstain from hitting people in the face, he was referred rather urgently by his teachers to a clinic school, where the aggressive behavior—along with some other disturbing problems—could be therapeutically addressed.

In addition to bullying and explosive rage, there were academic difficulties. William was never at all interested in classroom tasks and in fact had a rather distinct phobia in regard to school in general. He was frequently absent for reasons of asthma attacks and was more than once taken for emergency hospital treatment in connection with them. When he did come to school, the teacher could elicit little attention to any kind of work. William would turn sullenly away from what was going on in class, with a tight-lipped refusal to participate in what was happening. He often seemed quite withdrawn, and he stored up grudges against his classmates, only to explode into an assaultive attack at some minor offense in the play yard. He appeared to harbor some smoldering anger within. Unable to give or receive friendly feelings toward the other children, and hostile toward all adults, he attached himself to an older boy who reigned as chief aggressor of the playground and helped to instigate fights against newcomers and smaller children.

In the play therapy room, one could see immediately the same picture: a cautious, silent constriction alternating with erratic demonstrations of anger. In William's play with small cars, a fire engine and a tow truck would stop up the exit of a racetrack, as though to prevent something's getting out. Repeatedly, William would put all the small cars into a larger container and cautiously move the container in constricted circles around one part of the room, without saying a word.

On the other hand, there were bits of play that seemed to allude to the aggression and anger. William would set out little men facing a line-up of cars, and, one by one, he would "fire" the cars at the men, methodically "mowing them down." If there were any survivors, William would call in the larger Batman car, which would then complete the massacre. William added an interesting and puzzling detail to the scene: just before the men were killed off, he would run a small dump truck up to the doomed men and pretend to dump something in front of them. I could only wonder what he was unloading there, because William was not inclined to share his thoughts about these matters. However, he did enlighten me about another bit of play: when he hurled lumps of clay at an unbreakable mirror in the room, he explained to me that he was throwing that clay "at the devil, because he beats his wife."

Of Dough

Soon after William began coming to the playroom, he found something there that suddenly sparked his interest: his eye fell on some flour and salt dough, which lay on the doll table, and he picked it up and began to play with it. He squeezed it, patted it, cut it into tiny pieces, and made a big pile of the pieces on one side of the table. The next play session began and ended in the same way, and for some weeks William concerned himself almost exclusively with this material. He asked whether he might help me make it, and each time he would have a little ceremony of mixing the salt and flour with the water and stirring it and kneading it until it was the right consistency. His original reticence about coming to sessions gave way to unbridled enthusiasm, and he asked why he could not come every day. Something about that dough was making a connection with him.

One day, William thoughtfully pushed a piece of the dough into a tiny plastic cup, made a deep hole in it with his finger, and asked me whether I would keep it for him until it was dry. About the same time, he began to express interest in a baby doll and at each session picked up the nursing bottle to feed her, at times asking me if I would hold the baby and rock it for him. Long after I thought he had forgotten the dough-filled plastic cup, he requested it one day and decided to take it with him when he left. His teacher told me that in class he often removed the strange little toy from his desk and appeared to drink from it. Whatever the dough was meaning to him in the playroom, he clearly had devised a way to take it with him into the larger world.

A problem emerged in connection with the dough: William began actually to put it in his mouth and swallow it. I explained that he must not really eat it, that it was play-like food, and I exercised all my ingenuity in helping him pretend to eat as a substitute for eating.

However, I failed in this effort: he would—and did—eat the dough, in the classroom as well as in the playroom. His teacher was also unable to prevent this gastronomical offense.

As the therapist, I was caught in a dilemma. I knew I could not allow him to eat the dough, but it also did not seem right to take away something so important to him. Departing from a long-held conviction that only play-like food is appropriate in the therapy setting, I said to him one day, "William, you need something you can really put into your mouth, something it won't hurt you to eat. I am going to think about it." The following week, having conferred with his teacher, I came to the session prepared, I thought, with an ingenious solution. I asked him whether he might like to make a real cake, one that he could take to class with him and share with his friends. He was incredulous and ecstatic. At the next session, as he helped to mix the eggs and water and cake mix and bring to fruition this promised treasure, he was in a fever of joy. When he took it triumphantly to class, his generosity elicited gratitude and esteem from all sides, and the previous grandeur of "hitting people in the face" seemed to pale before his new wave of glory. His teacher and I congratulated ourselves for what appeared to be instantaneous success in this innovative departure from classical play therapy technique.

Alas, our joy was naive and premature, and it was soon followed by a crisis in which the entire therapeutic process seemed threatened. William came eagerly to the next session—ready to make another cake! What more understandable expectation in the wake of his newly won distinction than that it would continue as it had begun, with a permanent feast in the classroom provided by himself as benefactor. To anticipate a phrase from D. W. Winnicott, a British psychoanalyst from whom we will hear a great deal later on, William had experienced a long overdue moment of the "illusion of omnipotence." However, the illusion was very brief, and it was suddenly and cruelly punctured by the impingement of certain realities of school life.

When William learned that the cake baking was a one-time affair, especially given the fact that every child in the classroom now had to have a turn baking one, he fell into a sullen despair. He would not speak to me. He came to his sessions but would stand by the window looking out and would not play. Neither did he acknowledge any of my attempts to reflect on how he might be feeling nor my efforts to take responsibility for not having prepared him for the reality that the cake was to be a one-time event. He had thought, after all, that here was someone who had made something new and satisfying available to him, and, just as he was tasting the fruits of it, it was snatched away again. He was angry and desolate.

Only after some weeks of refusal to speak to me did there come a break in the ice. One day, as I was working at my desk, a paper was slipped under my door, and I heard young feet running quickly away. It was a letter, which William's teacher had helped him to print, a written account of a conversation that had taken place between the two of them. It read:

> Dorothy wouldn't let me make a cake. And I was mad at Dorothy because she wouldn't let me make a cake. That's why I was mad at Dorothy and that's the end.
>
> (Teacher: Are you still mad?)
> No.
> (Why? Why are you not mad now?)
> I don't know.
> (Do you feel bad or sad still?)
> No.
> (What would you like to tell Dorothy?)
> I am happy. Is about time I'm happy. That's the end. Cause I feel better, feel happy now I'm not mad at Dorothy. I hope she feel happy 'cause I'm not mad at Dorothy no more. That's the end.

William never explained to us how he had come to this resolution, but he had made his peace with the passing of a fantasy of limitless plenty, a disillusionment, all too sudden, that had given him pain. In our next session, we found a substitute for the real cake—something between real and play-like—in the form of an instant pudding mix we could pretend was cake mix. He accepted this substitute cheerfully, with only an occasional wistful references to the time we made a real cake. At the same time, since Easter was approaching, real eggs could be decorated and devoured, in turn serving in that endless series of substitutions for an original joy, that of the mother's breast, which for this child, for whatever reasons, had been insufficiently bountiful.

The child did not lose the experience of the cake, as we shall see later. Shortly after he had mastered the disappointment, his teacher told me that he had for the first time warmed to a story she had read to the children in class, and that he had requested that she read it over and over. The story was about a little boy "who couldn't grow up until he had done something wonderful."

Of Changes

In the days and weeks following the incident of the cake, with its aftermath of anger and reconciliation, William's teachers told me that they were seeing some rather remarkable changes in him. "There has been some break-through with him," they said; "he is a different child." They mentioned that he had somehow become more accessible and less angry. He had begun to show some affection toward them and allowed them to show some affection toward him. Whereas before he had not allowed himself to be touched in class, he now joined in the playtime rough-housing and even took part in a game of horse-back riding, with his male teacher as the horse. They also mentioned that William had begun to cry with real tears when he was upset or disappointed about something. When a therapy session had to be delayed one day, they reported that he had sat in the doorway and wept uncontrollably, sobbing as if his heart would break.

Further changes appeared. Following his interest in the story of the little boy "who couldn't grow up until he'd done something wonderful," William began to show a flickering interest in letters and words, as though he might have some use for those formerly alien tools. If the teacher would allow him a safe corner, where no one could watch, he even tackled some pages in his programmed reader. The fear of books seemed to be waning.

More remarkable still, perhaps, were the reports from the teachers that William was fighting less, was cooperating and even helping at lunch time, and had given up his status as chief bully. In the therapy room one day, he lined up all the wild animals and made a small car run down each one, in turn. He explained: "There is going to be a new street, and they are in the way."

Later on, I will return to this matter of William's aggression and its alleviation and attempt an interpretation of the changes.

Of Feeding with Books

William found, in addition to his feast of the cake, another source of nourishment, a source familiar to all wise parents and teachers; he discovered books.

In this clinic school, there were opportunities to go to the children's playground, or dining area, or day room in unscheduled times and to offer alternatives to fighting. I found that if I went to those scenes armed with a half-dozen books and a blanket, and sat down and waited, someone would come and ask for a story, and within a few moments I would be surrounded by chirping little chicks clamoring to be fed. By trial and error, I quickly learned which stories captured and held the children's interest and began to discover that the degree of their excitement was connected to the ways in which these stories touched on their own lives. Their growing fascination with the activity made clear that something quite important was going on with them; there was some magnetic attraction here that was reaching them at a deeper level than met the eye. Something about the tales themselves, or about my reading them, or both, was reaching them at an unconscious as well as at a conscious level. A symbolic connection made a bridge between the children and me through the dynamics of the story.

For some time, the undisputed favorite was Curious George (Rey, 1941), the lovable, good-bad little monkey who was always in trouble; whose special friend, the man in the yellow hat, who had found him in the jungle and cared for him, always appeared just when he needed help; who was always forgiven; and who frequently found himself a hero in the end. The listeners seemed to appropriate something for themselves in hearing about the little monkey; it was as though their own unruly impulses found acceptance along with those of George, and their demand for these stories was insatiable.

When Robert, the horse with the powerful sneeze, made his entrance, he quickly outstripped George as the undisputed favorite. The children could not hear enough about this horse, whose troublesome sneezing knocked down everyone and everything in his path. The identification with this offensive creature, who found relief from his own uncontrollable destructive reactions only when they proved to be useful in capturing some bank robbers, was so palpable that the children began to memorize the sequence of events that preceded the sneezes. They would shout together, in concert:

> And his nose began to itch
> And his eyes began to itch and
> KERCHOO!
> Everyone fell down flat!

The joy and enthusiasm that vibrated through the group in these moments were contagious. The children's responsiveness confirmed for me that the key to motivation for learning is emotional involvement, unconscious as well as conscious resonance with words and meanings that tell us something about ourselves. For these children, the issue was of course their own difficulty in controlling their destructive aggression. That a fellow sufferer could find such a favorable resolution of a problem as to have it used in catching bank robbers offered new hope to these children, who felt trapped in destructiveness.

The child, William, avoided for a long time this group reading situation. However, he was clearly taking note from a distance and, very gradually, he began to come closer, within ear-shot of the stories. That bad little monkey who always found forgiveness for his misdeeds, whose friend, "the man in the yellow hat," never failed him, and that horse, whose powerful sneeze made him a hero in the end, called to him so persuasively that William could no longer resist. Suddenly he left his play, came and sat down beside me on the blanket, and drank in the story.

Shortly afterwards, he began to eye the same books in the playroom but said nothing. He would look toward them and then look away. After some weeks, he again melted and picked up a book from the shelf, a book about a little lost bear that got found. He brought it to me and asked hesitantly, "Would you read it to me?"

With these words, William ushered in a phase of his treatment that was to last nearly a year. He abandoned himself utterly to the task of making up for all the long overdue feeding. His sessions hardly varied from that day until William was ready to leave the clinic school: each time he entered the room, he would ceremoniously gather together his supplies—the "cake-mix," the hard-boiled eggs, which had somehow remained essential to him, and put them in a large box. Then he would select a book and put the book in the box. He would then climb into the box himself. As he took up the cake-mix and started to eat, he would say, "Now please read me the story." At the end of the first story, he would ask for a second, and, at the end of the second, a third. William was clearly addicted to a new kind of nourishment.

Of the New Street

By now there were signs for all to see that something had happened with William that had radically altered his picture. The asthma had disappeared. He came eagerly to school, and the former freeze on learning tasks had undergone a massive thaw. His teachers, who in their own sphere ably facilitated this child's growth, reported that he had now an almost insatiable demand for work and simply reveled in it. In the course of making new assessments and evaluations for the next step, we learned that William's I.Q. score had jumped by sixteen verbal points in one year.

In the playroom, William was beginning to tell me about some of these victories. He told me he was learning to read and write. He was clearly getting competent at a number of things of which he was very proud, and he smiled when I reminded him that he had once said that he was mainly "good at hitting people in the face." There were few reports of fights, and William no longer qualified as an aggressive, impulse-ridden child in need of a clinic school. A place in a special program in the public school was obtained for him, and, some months after he had been in attendance there, his teacher wrote to me: "William is very polite, quiet, and well-behaved; he is working out nicely in the program. The academics are fine—in fact, he is one of our best kids."

William had been right when, finishing off those wild animals in the playroom, he had said that they were simply in the way now because there was going to be a new street. At this writing, the report from school is that he is still walking along that new street.

With full regard for the differences in these stories, we may ask the question, what do they hold in common?

We may say, first of all, that in each journey some changes in emotional life have taken place. Troublesome symptoms had interfered in the daily experience of each child: Amy had to "wear a mask" and spend a great deal of energy fending off bad feelings and keeping them out of awareness; John was compelled to fail and stay on the fringes of what was going on at school; William was under the tyranny of his own aggression. In the course of the therapeutic journeys the symptoms abated, and the children all seemed to be freed for new levels of growth.

A conspicuous common factor in the journeys is the children's use of symbol. In playing with toys, painting, molding something from clay, or manipulating dough, the children were expressing fantasy images in which they spontaneously sketched out and worked with their conflicts and needs. They communicated and addressed their deepest inner concerns through dramatic enactment.

A third common factor in the three journeys is that each of them occurred in the context of a relationship with a psychotherapist, with whom the child spent one hour a week, in a similar playroom, over a period of some two years.

The convergence of these three common factors in the journeys invites investigation. How do we understand the changes in the emotional life? What is the significance of the children's use of symbol in this change, and what is the significance of the relationship with the psychotherapist in the change? One way of stating the investigative question is: How are the child's use of symbol and the contextual relationship related to the therapeutic changes as described above?

In order to pursue this question, it will be useful to review some of the ways the changes could be understood from the standpoints of two major theoretical perspectives.

Chapter II

INVESTIGATION FROM THE STANDPOINTS OF TWO MAJOR THEORIES

FREUD

A contemporary Freudian approach to understanding what happened with the three children would center on the resolution of certain conflicts that were interfering with the children's potential for growth. The task of containing, regulating, and managing impulses are understood to be interfering with optimal development; troublesome symptoms, such as the constriction in Amy and John, are resulting from the conflict between containment and the stirring of libidinal and aggressive impulses that are striving for expression. As these conflicts are resolved in the course of the therapeutic work, the drives come increasingly under the power of the ego, the functioning of the ego is strengthened, and growth, which has been impeded, can proceed.

One specific way to reflect on what happened to Amy's wriggly worms and John's bank robbers and William's wild animals is to consider them from the perspective of Freud's notion of sublimation. In order to understand that idea, we will review briefly the theory that led to it.

Freud's early work drew on the idea of "psychic energy," which he understood to be sexual in nature, in order to explain most psychological phenomena. This early theory came to be known as the theory of the libido. Later he came to accept aggressive strivings along with the sexual ones, and current Freudian theory speaks simply of the libidinal and aggressive drives.

One important contribution from the libido theory, with its emphasis on sexuality, is its expansion of the meaning of "sexual" into a much wider sense than a simply genital one (1905, 1925, p. 38f.), though the lay perception of his theory, both in his own time and in our own, has not always recognized that fact. From Freud's point of view, sexual energy had a scope broad enough to include a vast range of phenomena not previously understood as sexual; his theory of the libido contributed the tools to illumine such apparently disparate occurrences as thumbsucking in children and the sobering presence in the world of a sex murderer.

The expansion from genital, reproductive sexual function in the narrow sense to the libido or sexual instincts in a wider sense, was in fact something like a blaze of electric light suddenly turned on in a room previously lit dimly by a candle or two. The illuminating quality derives from Freud's hitting on the nature of this force as composite, plastic, and mobile; it is not one thing, in other words, and it is not of one piece, nor does it have one function, nor one fate.

Sexuality derives from numerous tributary forces, such as different parts of the body and several partial instincts (e.g., pleasure in looking and being looked at and the active and passive forms of the instinct of cruelty), and is subject to excitation by a variety of routes, including muscular, affective, and intellectual processes. It is phylogenetically built up, having a different organization at different stages of child development; it is dissectible into aim (the act of satisfaction), object (the person or thing through which it is satisfied), and source. It is composite and subject to falling apart again into its components by a regression to a previous stage of its organization.

For example, such a falling apart into components of sexuality by regression may result in a "perversion," by which Freud meant an aberration of the sexual instinct from its integrated state in such a way that one or another of the partial instincts predominates, as in sadism or voyeurism. Another example would be deviations in regard to either aim or object of the sexual instinct, as in fetishism. An alternative to perversion, in this technical sense, Freud saw to be neurosis, or what he called the negative of perversion. Neurotics, in Freud's view, entertain the same deviations in the unconscious as "perverts" do in actuality, and it is these aberrations that are expressed in symptoms (1905, p. 165).

Freud thus demonstrated the relative ease with which the sexual instinct can accept substitutes for an original aim and/or an original object (thus enlightening the varieties of sexual choice in human experience), can reverse itself along a pathway, can separate itself out into its component partial instincts, and can be repressed into the unconscious mind and express itself as neurotic symptoms (substitute satisfactions and compromise formations). It can attach itself to one or another part of the mind and body, can be invested in other persons, or it can hover around the ego itself (1914). It can get stuck (fixated) in any of these loci, and it can, under certain circumstances get unstuck and reinvested in the most diverse ways, including being channeled into culturally useful forms, such as artistic and intellectual work; that is, it can be *sublimated*.

Freud first used the term *sublimation* in the *The Three Essays* in discussing the libidinal excitation of visual impression:

> It [sexual curiosity] can, however, be diverted ('sublimated') in the direction of art, if its interest can be shifted away from the genitals on to the shape of the body as a whole. It is usual for most normal people to linger to some extent over the intermediate sexual aim of a looking that has a sexual tinge to it; indeed, this offers them a possibility of directing some proportion of their libido on to higher artistic aims (1905, p. 156f.).

Further along in the same essay:

> Historians of civilization appear to be at one in assuming that powerful components are acquired for every kind of cultural achievement by this diversion of sexual instinctual forces from sexual aims and their direction to new ones—a process which deserves the name 'sublimation' (1905, p. 178).

Throughout Freud's work there are references to the placing of the sexual instinct, the libido, at the disposal of cultural productivity through a substitution of aim or object or both (1908a, 1909a, 1909b,

1909c, 1910, 1913a, 1914, 1917a, 1923, 1925, 1940). A representative statement would be:

> There are only two possibilities of remaining healthy when there is a persistent frustration of satisfaction in the real world. The first is by transforming the psychical tension into active energy which remains directed toward the external world and eventually extorts a real satisfaction of the libido from it. The second is by renouncing libidinal satisfaction, sublimating the dammed-up libido and turning it to the attainment of aims which are no longer erotic and which escape frustration (1912b, p. 232).

Also

> A certain kind of modification of the aim and change of the object, in which our social valuation is taken into account, is described as 'sublimation' (1933a, p. 97).

Again:

> Observation of men's daily lives shows us that most people succeed in directing very considerable portions of their sexual instinctual forces to their professional activity. The sexual instinct is particularly well fitted to make contributions of this kind since it is endowed with a capacity for sublimation: that is, it has the power to replace its immediate aim by other aims which may be valued more highly and which are not sexual (1910, p. 77f).

An important recurring emphasis in Freud's own treatment of sublimation was its special manifestation in art (1910, 1917b, 1924b). A significant passage on this theme reads as follows:

> For there is a path that leads back from phantasy to reality—the path, that is, of art. An artist is once more in rudiments an introvert, not far removed from neurosis. He is oppressed by excessively powerful instinctual needs.... Their constitution probably includes a strong capacity for sublimation and a certain degree of laxity in the repressions which are decisive for a conflict.... A man who is a true artist has more at his disposal. In the first place, he understands how to work over his day-dreams in such a way as to make them lose what is too personal about them and repels strangers, and to make it possible for others to share in the enjoyment of them. He understands, too, how to tone them down so that they do not easily betray their origin from proscribed sources. Furthermore, he possesses the mysterious power of shaping some particular material until it has become

a faithful image of his phantasy; and he knows, moreover, how to link so large a yield of pleasure to his representation of his unconscious phantasy that, for the time being, at least, repressions are outweighed and lifted by it (1917b, p. 375f.).

An Elaboration of Freud's Concept of Sublimation: Paul Ricoeur

Sublimation as a way of conceiving the children's therapeutic changes may be clarified by Paul Ricoeur's development and elaboration of this concept of Freud's (1970, 1974, 1976). Ricoeur's treatment of the idea is quite useful, in that it brings into the sphere of sublimation a great deal of Freud's work not previously called by that name, along a line of thought stemming from Freud's understanding of the dream. Ricoeur pointed out that Freud's treatment of the dream really serves as a model or paradigm of the "oneiric in general," or all that is veiled in human experience, in waking life as well as in sleep:

> Psychoanalysis is of value insofar as art, morality, and religion are analogous figures or variants of the oneiric mask. The entire drama of dreams is thus found to be generalized to the dimensions of a universal poetics (Ricoeur, 1970, p. 162).

This "veiled" experience Ricoeur explains as an endless derivative progression of instinctual vicissitudes, following Freud's dictum that

> Actually, we can never give anything up; we only exchange one thing for another. What appears to be a renunciation is really the formation of a substitute or surrogate (Freud, 1908b, p. 145).

He calls further to our attention Freud's thought:

> Might we not say that every child at play behaves like a creative writer, in that he creates a world of his own, or rather, re-arranges the things of his world in a new way which pleases him? It would be wrong to think he does not take the world seriously; on the contrary, he takes his play very seriously and he expends large amounts of emotion on it. The opposite of play is not what is serious but what is real. In spite of all the emotion with which he cathects his world of play, the child distinguishes it quite well from reality; and he likes to link his imagined objects and situations to the tangible and visible things of the real world. This linking is all that differentiates the child's play from 'phantasying'.

> The creative writer does the same as the child at play. He creates a world of phantasy which he takes very seriously—that is, which he invests with large amounts of emotion—while separating it sharply from reality. Language has preserved this relationship between children's play and poetic creation (Freud, 1908b, p. 143).

In drawing our attention to these passages, Ricoeur points to a continuum of the "oneiric in general," from the dream, to children's play, to fantasy, to poetry and creative writing, and other works of art: a progressive self-transformation of substitutes which can be understood as analogical to the dream and similarly deciphered through the unraveling of the dream work, as Freud describes it.

The special significance of Ricoeur's work for our understanding of what was going on with Amy, John, and William lies in the endeavor to show that these instinctual derivatives, from play to art, are not simply "the endless repetition of origins." He makes some very interesting observations regarding the progressive self-transformation of symbols in a telic direction. He points out, for example, that in the now famous incident of the "fort und da" game of Freud's young grandson, the child was not simply hallucinating wish fulfillment, but rather was attempting to gain mastery over an instinctual concern, namely object loss, or his mother's absence (Freud, 1920, p. 14f.). Similarly, drawing on Freud's treatment of Leonardo da Vinci, Ricoeur notes the following about the painting of the Mona Lisa:

> Leonardo's brush does not recreate the memory of the mother; it creates it as a work of art. That is the sense in which Freud could say that "in these figures Leonardo denied the unhappiness of his erotic life and has triumphed over it in his art." The work of art is thus both symptom and cure (1970, p. 174).

In this suggestion of Freud's that in the smile of the Mona Lisa the past is "denied and overcome" Ricoeur finds the clue that artistic creations "are not simply projections of the artist's conflicts, but the sketch of their solution.... The work of art goes ahead of the artist; it is a prospective symbol of his personal synthesis and of man's future, rather than a regressive symbol of his unresolved conflicts" (1970, p. 175).

Thus Ricoeur advances the hypothesis that the true meaning of sublimation is "to promote new meanings by mobilizing old energies initially invested in archaic figures" (1970, p. 175). The instinctual derivatives point us progressively forward toward further self-transformation; they do not simply point us back to the arché of infancy.

While Ricoeur's purpose in the passages above is primarily to illumine the nature of works of art, it appears to me that some of his insights are quite useful in pursuing the nature of the changes we observed in the children during the course of their play therapy. Specifically, he contributes the view that the symbolic fantasy of play (and art) does not simply reveal the instinctual underlayers, from which their energy derives, nor does it simply depict the conflict of these underlayers; rather, it provides a sketch for the solution to the conflicts in the mobilization of old energies in the promotion of new meanings. He suggests by his viewpoint that the child in play is "dreaming," in a sense, in such a way as to invest archaic forces into a progression of self-transformations that creates something new. Amy, John, and William could be said, then, to have redirected their instinctual strivings into what Freud called sublimations or what Ricoeur called new meanings.

It now seems clear that Freud's notion of sublimation, especially as it is elaborated by Ricoeur, is useful in accounting for the changes in the psychological experience of the children. But the question arises, what is it that makes sublimation happen in the particular context of play therapy? What are we dealing with in play therapy that a child's play *per se*, i.e., without the presence of the therapist, would not accomplish?

Freud stated more than once (e.g., 1917d, p. 455f.) that in order for the libido to be sublimated, there had to be a relatively free flow available to the ego. Otto Fenichel, who provided the definitive summarization and comprehensive text on Freudian theory (1940), stated that "Sublimations require an unchecked stream of libido just as a mill wheel needs an unimpeded and channeled flow of water. For this reason, sublimations appear after a repression has been removed" (p. 141). If this statement is true, it raises the question of how the supply of libido was made available to Amy, John, and William for their use in their new creations.

A clue to this question is offered by Freud's observations in discussing two phases of analytic work:

> In the first [phase], all the libido is forced from the symptoms into the transference and concentrated there; in the second, the struggle is waged

around this new object and libido is liberated from it. The change which is decisive for a favorable outcome is the elimination of repression in this renewed conflict, so that the libido cannot withdraw once more from the ego by flight into the unconscious. This is made possible by the alteration of the ego which is accomplished under the influence of the doctor's suggestion....Further light may perhaps be thrown on the dynamics of the process of cure if I say that we get hold of the whole of the libido which has been withdrawn from the dominance of the ego by attracting a portion of it on to ourselves by means of the transference (1917d, p. 455).

Freud appears to be emphasizing that the libido that is freed for sublimation is made available through a new object relationship—namely the transference to the analyst. Actually, is there not a close connection between what Freud is saying here and his later hypothesis about sublimation in *The Ego and the Id* (1923)? There he says that sublimation involved a re-routing of the libido through object relationship: a "setting up of an object in the ego," an internalization, or identification, thus desexualizing the libido and rendering it accessible for the ego's use (p. 45).

The transformation of object-libido into narcissistic libido which thus takes place obviously implies an abandonment of sexual aims, a desexualization—a kind of sublimation, therefore. Indeed, the question arises, and deserves careful consideration, whether all sublimation does not take place through the mediation of the ego, which begins by changing sexual object-libido into narcissistic libido and then, perhaps, goes on to give it another aim (p. 30f.).

In this somewhat opaque passage, the point of the matter seems to be that the process of sublimation is very closely allied to identification. Fenichel helps to clarify what Freud seems to be saying:

Sublimation is characterized by a) an inhibition of aim b) a desexualization c) a complete absorption of an instinct into its sequela, and d) by an alteration within the ego. All these qualities can also be seen in the results of certain identifications, as for example, in the process of formation of the superego. The empirical fact that sublimations, especially those that arise in childhood, depend upon the presence of models, upon incentives directly or indirectly supplied by the environment, corroborates Freud's assumption that sublimation may be intimately related to identification. Moreover, the cases of disturbance in the capacity to sublimate show that such an incapacity corresponds to difficulties in making identifications (1940, p. 142).

Investigations from the Standpoints of Two Major Theories

This connection between identifications—or setting up of objects within the ego—and sublimation of instinctual drives is important in understanding Amy, John, and William and what was happening with them in the course of their journeys. This view of Freud's places their sublimation of instinct clearly into the sphere of object relationship. Is there not here a clear connection between this understanding of sublimation and Freud's explanation of how the libido gets freed for sublimation in the course of analytic therapy? The libido that has been tied up in symptoms is loosened, released, and made available for new disposition by the ego "through attracting a portion of it onto ourselves by means of the transference" (Freud, 1917d, p. 455).

The question raised above—why it is that the sublimation in the children happens in a special way in the context of play therapy as distinguished from play per se—now has a reply. From the Freudian perspective, the sublimation of the instinctual drives happens in connection with a new object relationship: the transference onto the therapist of a portion of the libido formerly tied up in repression.

Thus, in the thought of Freud, I believe it to be demonstrated that the transformation or redistribution of libidinal and aggressive impulses into sublimations is a *relational* phenomenon.

JUNG

A second major theoretical perspective that may prove useful in understanding the psychological changes that appeared in the course of the journeys is that of Carl Gustav Jung. If we shift to the Jungian viewpoint and consider the questions raised above within its different frame of reference, what suggests itself as useful?

Perhaps if one could choose only one concept of Jung's as most cogent in describing the journeys, it might be that the children were involved in what he called "becoming one's own self" (Jung, CW, 7, Par. 266).[1] Something was happening to the children that resulted in their growth toward the actualization of potentialities that were latent in the psyche, somewhat analogous to the growing of a seed into a

---

[1] Because of the organization of the English translation of Jung's writings, citations from Jung will be made in the text by reference to the Volume Number and Paragraph in the Collected Works rather than by date of publication.

flower, "a process by which a man becomes the definite, unique being he in fact is" (Par. 267).

Jung viewed the entire course of life as a series of metamorphoses in human development, beginning with a first differentiation out of an unconscious matrix, out of a primitive identity (participation mystique), not only with the immediate parents but with an archaic heritage reaching back to the dawn of human existence. From this initial ground of being, or collective unconscious, the individual is involved for life in a struggle to gain progressive mastery over and independence from this original engulfment in an unconscious matrix without losing the life-giving sustenance of its resources (CW, 7, Par. 221-242).

Jung used certain vivid images to describe this life-long struggle to liberate one's self from the collective unconscious, who, like a Great Mother, feeds and sustains life and, at the same time, can threaten to overwhelm and swallow up the nascent ego. John's fantasies about bodies of water, with heroes in constant danger of being engulfed by them, come to mind in connection with this image of the Great Mother. Jung pointed to the universality of the hero image to illustrate the timeless necessity of the ego to emerge out of the belly of the dragon and embark on the progressively difficult tasks in the life-long, hazardous struggle towards achieving one's full stature (CW, 5, Par. 68f.). The heroes of fairy tales and myth illustrate this long struggle (von Franz, 1970; Bettelheim, 1976), and anyone who watches children's play witnesses the same timeless drama.

Jung's term for the development through life of one's inherent potentialities, the actualization of one's unique possibilities for growth, is *individuation*, and this is the comprehensive concept from which we may consider the children's journeys from the Jungian perspective. One way of understanding what happened to all three children is that they were somehow enabled to grow toward a higher level of development, toward a new degree of integration into conscious adaptation of the inner and outer worlds; or, in Jung's term, they were engaged in one small part of the life-long task of individuation. If we take this concept as central, what, according to Jung, is involved in the process of individuation?

The Transformation of Psychic Energy

In Jung's writing a major theme in the development of the concept of individuation is that of the transformation of psychic energy, and his use of that term needs to be clarified.

In the first place, Jung did not agree with Freud that psychic energy could be comprehended solely on the basis of instinctual strivings. For Jung this focus was much too narrow. He did not see psychic energy as a personally contained entity; rather, his observations of his patients and of his own psychic experiences led him to perceive the mind as an instrument through which autonomous psychic forces beyond it are felt, forces which sweep in upon us and are not automatically subject to consciousness, namely the collective unconscious:

> No, the collective unconscious is anything but an encapsulated personal system; it is sheer objectivity, as wide as the world and open to all the world. There I am the object of every subject, in complete reversal of my ordinary consciousness, where I am always the subject that has an object (CW, 9(1), Par. 11).

That the mind is the object of a larger subject, of dynamic springs of energy that have their own life, that attract, convince, fascinate, and overpower the conscious mind (CW, 9(1), Par. 11), Jung found to be true in his own experience. After his break with Freud, he underwent a severe emotional crisis. He began to submit himself, quite consciously, to the images and impulses of the unconscious and to confront and deal with the powerful contents with which he began to feel invaded in dreams and fantasies. He spoke of these intensive encounters in this way:

> I hit upon this stream of lava, and the heat of its fires reshaped my life. That was the primal stuff which compelled me to work upon it, and my works are a more or less successful endeavor to incorporate this incandescent matter into the contemporary picture of the world....the later details are only supplements and clarifications of the material that burst forth from the unconscious, and at first swamped me. It was the prima materia for a lifetime's work (Jung, 1961, p. 199).

Thus, Jung felt himself to be invaded by the world of the unconscious, and he set about to try to understand it on its own terms. This "stream of lava" image[2] is one way of encapsulating Jung's different picture of the psychic energy issue. A stream of lava is something that comes from beyond the merely personal; it happens to one; it denotes powerful and uncontrollable rushes of energy from without, and it is not subject to the tenuous controls of human consciousness. It denotes autonomous springs of energy that "come upon us like fate" (CW, 9(1), Par. 62).

These autonomous springs of energy Jung observed to give rise to certain universal themes and motifs and impulses to action that find expression in myths, fairy tales, religions, dreams, and fantasies in all cultures, and he called these dynamisms archetypes in line with the historical usage of that term he traced from antiquity (CW, 9(1), Par. 5f.). In our attempt to understand, from Jung's framework, the changes in Amy, John, and William, the importance of this part of the theory is that these autonomous forces, these dynamisms of the collective unconscious that give rise to thematic expression in the mind nudge the psyche toward its further development—toward its wholeness—toward its becoming what one is—toward, in short, individuation.

These archetypes are far from being of simply intellectual interest; they are vital forces that move in on the mind to correct and compensate for what is underdeveloped in consciousness, to push it toward its further advance. Erich Neumann, a Jungian, clarifies how normal human development is guided by these archetypal dominants that are crystallized in the personal unconscious. Speaking of stages of human development in their natural and cultural dimensions, he says:

> Although in our time this cultural sublimation of the natural transformations has been virtually lost, the natural, curative power of the unconscious has been very largely preserved in the healthy, normal man. Not only is he guided through the phases of life—though less so than primitive man—by his phylogenetic development, but moreover his whole life is molded by the compensatory action of the psyche with its tendency toward wholeness (Neumann, 1959, p. 156).

According to Jung's thought, this energic pushing of the psyche toward its further development involves a spontaneous symbol-making propensity that enables the conscious mind to have a "bridge" to the unconscious, and vice-versa, in such a way that the ego can

---

[2] Davidson (1979) draws attention to this image.

Investigations from the Standpoints of Two Major Theories 47

integrate what each offers to the progressive enlargement and wholeness of the psyche (the "transcendent function," in Jung's term).

> The avowed purpose of this [symbolic] involvement is to integrate the statements of the unconscious, to assimilate their compensatory content, and thereby produce a whole meaning which alone makes life worth living and, for not a few people, possible at all (CW, 14, Par. 756).

It is the dynamic springs of energy from the collective unconscious—the archetypes—which give rise to fantasies in the personal unconscious that have a constructive effect. Neumann explains it this way:

> These fantasies give the blocked personality a new direction, start the psychic life on a new advance, and cause the individual to become productive. A relation to the primordial image, the archetypal reality, brings about a transformation that must be designated as productive (1959, p. 158).

To summarize: from Jung's standpoint, psychic energy is far from being synonymous with instinctual drives as personally understood. It derives, in fact, from dominant springs of energy beyond the personal unconscious that act on the individual psyche and urge it toward wholeness and development in the direction of "becoming what one is."[3]

The concept of psychic energy was thus for Jung a broader one than it was for Freud. While Jung agreed with much of Freud's understanding of instinctual, personal strivings that lead an autonomous, independent life in the unconscious and wield powerful effects on the psyche (CW, 8, Par. 204f.), and while he agreed that there are sexual instincts, he did not accept the idea that they constitute the entire meaning of the libido. For Jung the libido is the energy of the life process in its entirety:

---

[3] An aspect of Jung's view of psychic energy that will not be discussed here is his view that it is underlain by the nature of opposites: polar tension as the source of psychic energy, or *enantriodromia*. He uses this term to designate the play of opposites in the course of events, the view that everything that exists turns to its opposite (Heraclitus). Jung used the term to describe the phenomenon that, whenever an extreme, one-sided tendency dominates conscious life, an equally powerful counterposition is built up, which eventually breaks through the conscious control (CW, 8, Par. 709).

> Libido as psychic energy naturally has these attributes too [elements of direction, regularity, and an ordered path or process]; the concept of energy necessarily includes the idea of a regulated process, since a process always flows from a higher potential to a lower. It is the same with the libido concept, which signifies nothing more than the energy of the life process. Its laws are the laws of vital energy. Libido as an energy concept is a quantitative formula for the phenomena of life, which are naturally of varying intensity. Like physical energy, libido passes through every conceivable transformation; we find ample evidence of this in the fantasies of the unconscious and in myths....Hence it is simply the expression of flowing and self-manifesting energy (CW, 6, Par. 355).

In a carefully developed paper on this subject (CW, 8, Par. 1-130), Jung placed his own view of the libido in the train of the classical use of the term in Greek thought and differentiated his own views from those of Freud, which seemed to make sexuality synonymous with libido:

> His [Freud's] concept of sexuality includes not only the physiological sexual processes but practically every stage, phase, and kind of feeling or desire. This enormous flexibility makes his concept universally applicable, though not always to the advantage of the resulting explanations (CW, 8, Par. 106).

Jung goes on to say in this passage that Freud's concept equates a symptom with a work of art and fails to distinguish between them.

However, Jung expressed appreciation for Freud's work on the idea of equivalences and substitutions for psychic energy and noted the usefulness of the idea that a sum of libido "has gone somewhere else," for example, from the conscious to the unconscious mind (CW, 8, Par. 35). He also agreed that, when a sum of libido has been transferred from the conscious to the unconscious mind, there is a similarity in the unconscious equivalent to what had been conscious and was then repressed. He developed this idea of equivalence, or substitution, through what he called the "canalization" of libido:

> I mean by this a transfer of psychic intensities or values from one content to another, a process corresponding to the physical transformation of energy [illustrated by the transformation of steam into motion]. Similarly, the energy of certain psychological phenomena is converted by suitable means into other dynamisms.

Investigations from the Standpoints of Two Major Theories 49

Continuing this idea, he makes the analogy to physical transformation:

> The living body is a machine for converting the energies it uses into other dynamic manifestations that are their equivalents. We cannot say that physical energy is transformed into life, only that its transformation is the expression of life (CW, 8, Par. 80).

The transformation of the psychic energy, says Jung, is achieved by its canalization into an analogue. "Just as a power station imitates a waterfall and thereby gains possession of its energy, so the psychic mechanism imitates the instinct and is thereby enabled to apply its energy for special purposes" (CW, 8, Par. 83).

The conversion into an analogue of the original instinct is the connection to Jung's emphasis that it is the *symbol* that is the transformer of the libido (CW, 8, Par. 88f.).

> I have called a symbol that converts energy a "libido analogue." By this I mean an idea that can give equivalent expression to the libido and canalize it into a form different from the original one (CW, 8, Par. 92).

> In practical work with our patients, we come upon symbol-formation at every turn, the purpose of which is the transformation of libido (CW, 8, Par. 93).

Jung asserted that this transformation of libido through symbol is a process that has been going on since the beginnings of humanity, and that it can be demonstrated amply from mythology, of which the symbols can be shown to be very closely connected to dream symbols. He pointed out that the nature of symbols as transformers of energy can be illustrated by certain archaic rites, such as the primitive's charging himself with power by rubbing his fetish (CW, 8, Par. 92).

Jung emphasized the idea that *transformation* of the libido, which involves the transfer of libido from one area of the psyche to another and its metamorphosis into all manner of new forms, is the work of the psyche in expressing ultimate concerns. It is an authentic part of psychic existence and cannot be regarded as derivative. Therefore, for Jung, the concept of sublimation becomes void, and he replaces it with the concept of transformation (CW, 5, Par. 190f.; 8, Par. 92f.). Transformation implies a liberation of creative forces that may then be utilized in the service of the greater-than-personal objectives; it is to be distinguished from Freud's notion of "change of aim and object of an instinct" as its fundamental nature.

Libido, then, in Jung's view is a of neutral energy, which undergoes transformation via the symbol. While the concept of symbol will be dealt with more fully in the next chapter, it will illumine the issue of the transformation of libido to mention at this point how Jung described the symbol as the bearer of energy, which wrests specific quantities of libido from the sphere of the unconscious to that of the conscious mind, rendering the energy usable to the ego. In "The Technique of Differentiation Between the Ego and the Figures of the Unconscious" (CW, 7, Par. 341f.), he explained the "rescuing" effect of fantasy images in releasing amounts of libido from the grip of the unconscious mind. In describing, for example, a situation of psychic depression, he says:

> The unconscious has simply gained an unassailable ascendancy: it wields an attractive force that can invalidate all conscious contents—in other words, it can withdraw libido from the conscious world, and thereby produce a "depression,"...But as a result...we must...expect an accumulation of...libido...in the unconscious....

> And we can only release it from the grip of the unconscious by bringing up the corresponding fantasy images. That is why...we give the unconscious a chance to bring its fantasies to the surface....But because he gave his mood a chance to express itself in an image, he succeeded in converting at least a small amount of libido, of unconscious creative energy in eidetic form, into a conscious content and thus withdrawing it from the sphere of the unconscious (CW, 7, Par. 344-349).

Jung emphasized, however, that in order for a fantasy image to be effective in rescuing libido from the unconscious, it is necessary that one participate actively in the fantasy rather than passively observing, and he developed a method of enabling his patients to confront and integrate their own symbolic figures, a method that he called active imagination (CW, 8, 131-193).

This approach appears to bear marked similarity to what children do spontaneously in play therapy. Freud observed that when people grow up and stop playing with toys, they simply give up the visible, tangible objects associated with their fantasies (1908b, p. 144f.). Jung's method of active imagination appears to reestablish access to the unconscious by concrete images reminiscent of the way children use toys.[4]

In the pursuit of ways of understanding what was happening with Amy, John, and William in the playroom, we would regard the children's symbolic play, from the Jungian framework, as a transformation of psychic energy. It is as though the very act of creating an image, whether it be a house, or a battle scene, or a rescue mission, or a lump of dough, or a clay figure, or any other spontaneous rendition from the child's inner world, wrests something from the unconscious and gives the child access to it in a new way. According to this view, "Image and meaning are identical; as the first takes shape, so the latter becomes clear. Actually the pattern needs no interpretation; it portrays its own meaning" (CW, 8, Par. 802). Spontaneous forces working on the psyche have somehow moved the ego into transforming libido into new forms in the service of "becoming what one is."

The question arises, if indeed the therapeutic journeys can be understood as a transformation of psychic energy in this sense, what caused it to happen in the playroom with the therapist? Why did it happen there instead of somewhere else?

Symbolic Play in the Jungian Framework: Its Relation to the Inner World and the Human Environment

As indicated above, Jung regarded the psyche to be subject to forces beyond its personal dimensions. He asserted that the ego, the center of

---

[4] Paolo Aite, a Jungian analyst who practices in Rome, has offered a very interesting account of the use of sand play with an adult patient. He distinguishes between 'imaginative activity' and 'active imagination' on the basis of the degree of ego participation involved in the use of the images sketched out in the sand and also raises an interesting issue as to the relationship between transformative and defensive use of imagination. His use of a passage from Jung (CW, 8, p. 189) that compares consciousness to "an archipelago of islands which rise out of the sea and little by little converge to form a continent" suggests one way to conceptualize what the children were doing in their symbolic journeys. "Fragments of consciousness being transformed and tending to unite in relation to an image" is Aite's formulation (1978, p. 332).

consciousness, is subject to a higher referent that impinges on it and pushes it toward its own fulfillment:

> But, just as our free will clashes with necessity in the outside world, so also it finds its limits outside the field of consciousness in the subjective inner world, where it comes into conflict with the facts of the self. And just as circumstances or outside events "happen" to us and limit our freedom, so the self acts upon the ego like an *objective occurrence* which free will can do very little to alter (CW, 9(2), Par. 9). [Italics his.]

This concept of Jung's, the concept of the Self, is somewhat difficult and elusive. Without attempting to do justice to the idea in its entirety, I will for our present purpose call it the latent wholeness in the personality that guides the unfolding of its inherent potentialities.

Dorothy Davidson, a British analyst, has presented in an article on "Playing and the Growth of Imagination," the idea of "an original wholeness lying within the small body and mind of the human baby" (1979, p. 32), which relates Jung's theory of the self as "ground plan," Michael Fordham's "blue print for maturation," and Erikson's thought about epigenetic development.

> We could say that it seems as if the roots for the whole range of human experience and emotion are potentially there in the new-born baby....He is like a rudimentary little theatre complete with inbuilt *dramatis personae*....

She draws our attention to Erikson's contribution in this connection:

> Whenever we try to understand growth, it is well to remember the epigenetic principle which is derived from organisms *in utero*. Somewhat generalized, this principle states that anything that grows has a ground plan, and that out of this ground plan the parts arise, each part having its time of special ascendancy, until all the parts have arisen to form a functioning whole. At birth the baby leaves the chemical exchange of the womb for the social exchange system of his society where his gradually increasing capacities meet the opportunities and limitations of his culture...
>
> It is important to realize that in the sequence of his most personal experiences the healthy child, given a reasonable amount of proper guidance, can be trusted to obey inner laws of development, laws which create a succession of potentialities for significant interaction with those

persons who tend and respond to him and those institutions which are ready for him. While such interaction varies from culture to culture it must remain 'within the proper rate and proper sequence' which governs all epigenesis. Personality can therefore be said to develop according to steps pre-determined in the human organism (Erikson, 1968, p. 92f.).[5]

Davidson states the hypothesis that the baby's creative, symbolic play must be understood as developing in relation both to the inner world, the intra-psychic potentiality present from the first—the "rudimentary little theatre"—and to the immediate human environment, namely the mother who is now external to the baby.

> She is a mother who has reached that point in her own physical and psychological development which enables her to hold and feed her baby, physically with milk and psychologically with responses matched to the baby's reaching out (Davidson, p. 33).

The details of this early maternal environment as fundamental to the development of the infant's creative potential will be the subject of Chapter V. For the present, it is enough to say that, from the Jungian perspective, the transformation of psychic energy through the symbol, in the service of "becoming what one is," happens in part spontaneously, as a result of unconscious forces acting on the ego and pushing it toward the actualization of a ground plan for wholeness, and in part as a result of the adequacy of the immediate human environment, which provides its original matrix.

Two Jungian authors who have stressed the significance of the early fusion with the parents in the psychological growth of the child are Frances Wickes (1927) and Dora Kalff (1971). In the introduction to Wickes' book, Jung commented that "The prime psychological condition is one of fusion with the psychology of the parents, an individual psychology being only potentially present."

Wickes demonstrated from a life-time of therapeutic work with children the truth of Jung's statement. The continuity of the unconscious of parents and children underlies many emotional disturbances in the children, and it is manifest in their dreams and fantasies.

---

[5] Michael Fordham (1969) connects Jung's theory of archetypes to Spitz's "organizers" in the first year, Klein's "unconscious fantasy operating from birth," and Piaget's "innate schemata."

> The participation mystique, or primitive identity, causes the child to feel the conflicts of the parents and to suffer from them as if they were its own (Jung, CW, 18, Par. 217).

Dora Kalff (1971) presents a detailed account of play therapy with three children, interpreted from a Jungian perspective. The children spontaneously engaged in symbolic expressions of their inner depths and arrived, quite without interpretation, to the solution of their own psychic problems and to the alleviation of their symptoms. Mrs. Kalff understood the children to be actualizing their own inner pattern for wholeness through the energy-laden pictures from the inner self, and she understood this growth to happen in the way that it did partly because of the "free and sheltered space" she was able to offer them in her own presence. Describing what she felt to be the effects of the transference relationship, she stated that there was thus created, through the relationship of confidence, a *participation mystique*, "which creates the situation of the first phase, that of mother-child unity. This psychic situation establishes an inner peace which contains the potential for the development of the total personality, including its intellectual and spiritual aspects" (1971, p. 17).

Thus it is clear that, from the Jungian perspective also, the transformation of libidinal energy involves a certain kind of relatedness to the immediate human environment. While there is an intra-psychic ground plan for wholeness, and, while there are spontaneous urges on the psyche that give rise to symbolic creativity in the service of growth, there is also a human matrix in relation to which all this must come into play (Davidson, 1971, p. 33).

Erich Neumann (1973) presents us with a startling comment that appears to connect these two foci, the inner and the outer:

> As we have seen, the development of the personality leads gradually to the independence of the ego and consciousness which liberate themselves from the shelter and clinging embrace of the unconscious of the Great Mother. In liberating itself, the ego grows away from the unconscious which is its nurturing soil. *The security and healthiness of this development depends on a successful primal relationship, that is, on a positive relation between mother and child, which is identical with the relationship between Self and ego, the unconscious and consciousness* (p. 181). [Italics mine.]

This statement would seem to be very significant for the present pursuit of the connection between creative symbolization and the relational context in which it occurs. Neumann seems to be saying that from the Jungian viewpoint the relationship of the ego and the unconscious matrix out of which it must grow, its Great Mother, cannot be distinguished from the matrix of the primal relationship between the child and the actual mother. While Jung says that "The unconscious is infinitely greater than the mother and is only symbolized by her,..." (CW, 5, Par. 450), the connection between the two suggests an inseparability between the inner and outer contexts for the transformation of psychic energy; that is, that the journey from unconscious to conscious—the transformation of the libido via the symbol, described above—derives initially from the maternal relationship as representative of the unconscious. This thought will be explored more fully in the next chapter in connection with the development of an hypothesis that the symbol arises between people, that it is a relational matter.

If Neumann's statement is true, namely that we cannot distinguish between the primal mother-child unity and the relationship between Self and ego, unconsciousness and consciousness, then it would seem that we have arrived at a conclusion not altogether different from that point at which we left the Freudian metaphor, namely that Freud came to see sublimation as dependent on object relations and as closely related to identification. It seems that Jung's point of view about the transformation of psychic energy in the course of "becoming what one is" also involves an identification, namely a primitive identity with the mother as the representative of the Great Mother, the Unconscious.

We have thus seen that both from the perspective of Freud's thought about sublimation of instinctual sexual and aggressive impulses and from that of Jung's treatment of the transformation of psychic energy, symbolic creativity cannot be separated from a context of human relationship. There are no doubt implications of this inseparability for understanding why the children in Chapter I changed in the ways that they did. In order to push this question further, I want now to investigate the two foci separately, that is, the focus of symbolic creativity and the focus of relationship. The next chapter will take up the question of the beginnings and development of symbolic expression in childhood; then we will explore in some detail the relational context.

Chapter III

THE BEGINNING AND DEVELOPMENT OF SYMBOLIC EXPRESSION IN CHILDHOOD

When and why does a child start to use symbols? What is their purpose for the child? In order to explore this question, I am going to offer a working hypothesis, namely that the symbol itself arises in the encounter between people, that is, that it is a relational phenomenon.

In light of so many widely divergent meanings attached to the word symbol, it is of course necessary to pause for definitions and to specify how I am going to use the term in the present context.

Symbolism, for Freud, had a very restricted function, and the Freudian school of psychoanalysis is still heavily influenced by his doctrine about it. The classic statement on this view of the matter was made by Ernest Jones (1916). In this paper, Jones distinguished between the wide meaning of symbolism, which includes anything of a figurative nature, that is, where something stands for something else, and the psychoanalytic meaning, in which symbolism "always constitutes a regression to a simpler mode of apprehension" (p. 199); always represents ideas of the self, the immediate blood relative, or the phenomena of birth, love, and death (pp. 169-170); and always involves the psychical repression of the affective and conative processes attached to the symbolized ideas (p. 182).

> Only what is repressed is symbolized. Only what is repressed needs to be symbolized. This conclusion is the touchstone of the psycho-analytical theory of symbolism (Jones, 1916, p. 183).

As already noted in Chapter II, Jung's understanding of the function of symbolism is in striking contrast to this position. For Jung, the symbol-making propensity in the human psyche provides a bridge between the conscious mind and the unconscious mind so as to facilitate the energic pushing of the psyche toward its further development. It is via the symbol that the ego has access to the riches of the collective unconscious, and it is the symbol that serves as the transformer, as the converter by analogue, of the libido. To review:

> The avowed purpose of this [symbolic] involvement is to integrate the statements of the unconscious, to assimilate their compensatory content, and thereby produce a whole meaning which alone makes life worth living and, for not a few people, possible at all (CW, 14, Par. 756).

Thus, Jung's view of the symbol is that it bears energy in a forward direction, in contrast to Jones' emphasis that it "always constitutes a regression to a simpler mode of apprehension":

> With the birth of the symbol, the regression of the libido into the unconscious ceases. Regression changes into progression, blockage gives way to flowing, and the pull of the primordial abyss is broken (CW, 6, Par. 445).

Parenthetically, it is interesting to note that the division of mind on this issue was quite explicit and heated when Jones wrote his article. Jones made a biting reference to Jung's view of symbolism,

> ...by which is meant the mystical, hermetic, or religious doctrine that is supposed to be contained in the symbol,...the ultimate ideal which is supposed to be symbolized by it....Along this path the post psychoanalytic school loses itself in a perfect maze of mysticism, occultism, and theosophy, into which I do not propose to penetrate (Jones, 1916, p. 203f.).

Paul Ricoeur's view of symbolism, as already noted, offers a synthesis between these two opposing positions regarding the retrogressive function of the symbol. He acknowledges the archaic, instinctual underlay of the symbol, in agreement with the Freudian position, but maintains that each symbol takes up a preceding one "to deny and overcome it," so that there is a progressive self-transformation of symbols in a telic direction:

> Since one and the same fantasy can carry two opposed vectors, a regressive vector which subjects the fantasy to the past, and a progressive vector which makes it an indicator of meaning....That the regressive and progressive functions can coexist in the same fantasy is intelligible in Freudian terms. Leonardo's vulture fantasy is a first transfiguration of the vestiges of the past: *a fortiori*, a true work of art like the Giaconda is a creation in which, in Freud's own words, the past is "denied and overcome" (Ricoeur, 1970, p. 539).

Ernst Cassirer contributed in his work on the *Philosophy of Symbolic Forms* a most comprehensive and enlightening view of symbolism. His insight into the nature of language was the means of differentiating symbolization as a legitimate mode of thought in its own right, as distinguished from its previous relegation in the philosophy of knowledge to the secondary sphere of superstition and the ignorance of myth. Symbolic forms, for Cassirer, provide the means of the apprehension of reality. Suzanne Langer explains Cassirer's departure from this traditional ascribing of a secondary status to symbolism relative to the sphere of facts and orderly thought:

> Here he was helped by a stroke of insight, the realization that language, man's prime instrument of reason, reflects his myth-making tendency more than his rationalizing tendency. Language, the symbolization of thought, exhibits two entirely different *modes* of thought. Yet in both modes the mind is powerful and creative. It expresses itself in different forms, *one of which is discursive logic, the other, creative imagination.*
>
> Human intelligence begins with conception, the prime mental activity; the process of conception always culminates in symbolic expression. A conception is fixed and held only when it has been embodied in a symbol. So the study of symbolic forms is a key to the forms of human conception. The genesis of symbolic forms—verbal, religious, artistic, mathematical, or whatever modes of expression there be—is the odyssey of the mind (Langer, 1946, p. viiif.). [Italics in text.]

There has been, in psychoanalytic literature, increasing recognition that the restriction of symbolism to its role in repression and defense—to its regressive aspects—is unnecessary and misleading.

Marion Milner (1952) reviewed the psychoanalytic use of symbolism and concluded that a broader conception of it is called for. She acknowledged the pertinence of Melanie Klein's view that symbolization is the basis of all talents, "that is, it is the basis of those skills by which we relate ourselves to the world around us" (Milner, 1952, p. 181). She also noted that an acceptance of the wider implications of the use of symbolism is more useful in relating psychoanalysis to other fields of intellectual work and is more in line with the practice of psychoanalysis itself, which, after all, asks the patient to utilize the "symbolic" relationship to the analyst as the very essence of the work.

In general, there is a wider acceptance of the view that "symbolization is a general capacity of the mind which is based on perception and which may be used either by the primary or the secondary process" (Rycroft, 1956, p. 137). It has become clear that the ability to use symbols is a definitive aspect of the development of the ego (Milner, 1952; Modell, 1968; Winnicott, 1971; Rodrigué, 1956), and, indeed, that the capacity to symbolize is the distinguishing characteristic of human beings:

> Clinical data supports the thesis that man is uniquely the symbol-using organism and is distinguished from the rest of nature and animal life by this fact (May, 1961, p. 20f.).

Erich Neumann, articulating Jung's perspective, makes a still stronger statement:

> Only if we recognize that symbols reflect a more complete reality than can be encompassed in the rational concepts of consciousness can we appreciate the full value of man's power to create symbols. To regard symbolism as an early stage in the development of the rational, conceptual consciousness involves a dangerous underestimation of the makers of symbols and of their functions without which the human species would be neither capable nor worthy of living (Neumann, 1959, p. 170).

Rollo May, an Existentialist, has supported this view that symbolizing is a capacity which characterizes the human being's relationship to the world. He cited evidence from Kurt Goldstein's work with wartime victims of brain injury, who had lost the capacity to relate themselves to their world in terms of symbols as a result of actual physical loss of parts of the cerebral cortex. "To have a self and a world

The Beginning and Development of Symbolic Expression

are correlates of the same capacity, and it was precisely this capacity that in these patients was impaired. They had lost the capacity to transcend the immediate concrete situation, to abstract, to think and live in terms of the possible" (May, 1961, p. 20).

May and others have noted that the capacity to use symbols, including language, arises developmentally at the time when conscious ego is differentiated from the unconscious, when self begins to be aware of the distinction between itself and the non-self, when inner and outer replaces the original undifferentiated state (Milner, 1952; Modell, 1968; Rodrigué, 1956; Rycroft, 1956; Winnicott, 1971). In the psychoanalytic treatment of children, I have been able to observe in more than one case the sudden emergence of the ability to make use of symbols; I will say more about that occurrence below.

Having reviewed, then, some of the different emphases in regard to the meaning and function of symbol that are found in the literature, I want to state what symbol has come to mean in my own thinking. The children's journeys have left me with the certainty that their use of symbol far exceeded the regressive and defensive. It involved the multi-layered condensation and displacement that Freud identified in the dream work (1900), but I think that Jung's perception of a deeper dimension to the use of symbol was also borne out by the children: they were expressing in the symbolic language something that was as yet unknown and unknowable to them in rational, conceptual terms, and they were using the symbol in a telic direction, as both Jung and Ricoeur stated it. I came to feel that the symbol provided for the children some life-giving medium, which may come progressively to light in the course of the present inquiry. At this point, I can make a tentative statement as to my perception of their use of symbol.

Amy, John, and William seemed to be expressing in their symbolic activity what I would describe as signs of new levels of being, and their own fantasy creations spoke their own messages more clearly than any interpretation of them that could be made. They did not denote one particular, identifiable meaning, rather they *connoted*[1] a mingling of realities and meanings for the child that were not only

---

[1] I am indebted to Barry Ulanov for this formulation in his paper, "Sublimation and the Boundaries of the Self": "All is connotation; denotation is only the thinnest introduction to the forests of symbol, the first of an endless series of veils to be removed in the processes of revelation" (p. 7).

"overdetermined," as Freud put it, but also irreducible to explication because they were themselves the most concise expression possible of something not yet known. They were clearly "under the sign of a new being," to use Gaston Bachelard's phrase (1958, p. xxv) and were "great with things to come," to use Suzanne Langer's (1953, p. 306). Examples of this sign of new being are Amy's series of houses, each "nobler than the last," her smiling snail with its spiraling chambers, John's new roads, and William's new street. To attempt to unravel the mystery of these symbols would be to lose something the child is saying, because each of them knits into a cohesive unit many meanings and represents something new in the child, of which the symbol is the most complete statement the child can make.

Of course, we can point to certain things the symbol may represent for the child: it points to the instinctual underlayers, as Freud saw; it transforms, by analogue, libido from the unconscious to the conscious sphere and gives the ego access to it in a new way, as Jung saw; it connects the child to the object world and all of reality, as Melanie Klein, D. W. Winnicott, and many others saw.

My own thought about the matter, in addition to all of these accurate perceptions, is that the symbolic play is in some way a means of appropriation of certain qualities of relationship, which I am going to investigate. It is the means by which the parent, or therapist, or some other significant person, in simplest terms, is "eaten," and by which the child is nourished. It is the symbol by which the children incorporate the vital force that is present in the other—for example, William's dough—, and it is the symbolic play by which they express, through "miniatures of vital impulse" (Bachelard, 1958, xxiii), their own enlarged boundaries, their own discoveries of parts of themselves previously unrealized or split off by repression; by which their own life force becomes mobilized into new creations through its being kindled in relationship.

I want to explore the idea that this particular human capacity to symbolize actually begins, arises, in the encounter between people, that it is relational in its essential nature.

Let us begin with the work of D. W. Winnicott, a British psychoanalyst, who had been a pediatrician. While Winnicott is going to be discussed in some detail at a later point, he is important to us here because he connects us to the one common theme found in virtually every serious treatment of the subject of symbolism, namely that *the symbol is the universal mediation between ourselves and external reality* (Cassirer, 1946, p. 8f.; Eliade, 1958; Gertz, 1958, p. 205f.; Jung, CW, e.g., Vol. 5; May, 1961; Richardson, 1955, p. 2f.; Ricoeur, 1970, p. 10; Van der Leeuw, 1963; Tillich, 1961). This common emphasis among all these authors can be summarized by a statement made by Rollo May:

> ...The symbol is a "bridging act," a bridging of the gap between outer existence (the world) and inner meaning, and it arose out of man's capacity to separate inner meaning and outer existence (May, 1961, p. 21).

Cyril Richardson, a church historian, made the point this way:

> Indeed, most of reality is not accessible to us without symbols; for it is by symbols that we come into contact with it. What the symbol does is to give reality meaning so that we can participate in it (1955, p. 2).

It has been the special contribution of D. W. Winnicott to explore the intermediate area between what is inner and subjective and what belongs to the outer, objective world. He observed that an infant who is fortunate enough to have what he calls "good-enough mothering," that is, a mothering person who can relate to the infant in such a way that the baby's needs are adequately met (Chapter V), is able to appropriate a rudimentary "symbol," that is, a "transitional object," something that is not "all me," nor is it something "all out there," but from the standpoint of the baby, something that has qualities of both. This something can be a teddy bear, or a part of a blanket, or even the baby's own thumb, but the distinguishing factor is that *it stands for something*. What it stands for is part of the mother, namely the breast: for the first time, a rudimentary symbol—the use of something to stand for something else—is employed *in the context of the very first relationship*.

Winnicott makes clear that an infant can employ the transitional object, this embryonic symbol, when the other person is adapted to the baby's needs completely enough for the baby to experience the illusion of omnipotent control over the breast, an illusion made possible by the overlap of what the mother supplies (an external reality) with the infant's own capacity to create (the inner conception). In this experience of illusion, born out of the earliest relatedness, Winnicott sees the roots of religion, and all creative endeavor, those spheres of life that are not subject to external verification, and which exist in the inbetween space between inner and outer:

> I am therefore studying the substance of *illusion*, that which is allowed to the infant, and which in adult life is inherent in art and religion, and yet becomes the hallmark of madness when an adult puts too powerful a claim on the credulity of others....We can share a respect for *illusory experience*, and if we wish we may collect together and form a group on the basis of the similarity of our illusory experience. This is a natural root of grouping among human beings (1971, p. 3).

Thus, in Winnicott's work, both the genesis and the development of symbolic life are seen to lie in human relationship. It is also noteworthy that group experience, or relatedness and encounter beyond the primary, one-to-one relationship, is seen here in conjunction with shared symbolic experience. It is also pertinent for our present inquiry that, in the absence of human relationship adequate to the infant's needs, there will be impairment of the child's ability to utilize symbols.

Clinical data from the work of Emilio Rodrigué, an Argentine analyst, illuminates the earliest processes of symbol formation. His autistic patient, Raul, moved out of his self-enclosed world in his play through an initial experience of a water basin clearly experienced as the mother's breast (an *equivalent* use of the symbol), to the use of a lampshade as a *representation* of the mother's breast. The analyst made clear that the relationship with the child made progress in line with the child's growing capacity to project onto external objects his internal symbolic material, which capacity grew along with his progressive ability to comprehend his separateness from the object:

> Every move he made towards that position [being able to bear the separateness of the object] brought in a constellation of symbols, which were ever richer in meaning and embraced an ever-wider range of objects and interests (1956, p. 156).

From this point of view, the symbol arises in conjunction with the necessity to come to terms with "what is out there that is not me," the prospect of losing the object as a result of "it's not being me." It is precisely at this juncture that a recalling, a "re-presentation" becomes necessary; prior to the acceptance of separation of self and other, we are speaking of an omnipotent, magical level of symbolization that is tantamount to "equivalence" as opposed to "representation." At the point of self-other differentiation, however, "every aspect of the object, every situation that has to be given up in the process of growing gives rise to symbol formation" (Rodrigué, p. 157).

This distinction between the symbolic as *equivalent* to and the symbolic as *representative of* is an important one; it has been recognized as the distinguishing factor between magical, primitive, omnipotent thought and true re-presentation (Modell, 1968; Winnicott, 1971; Rodrigué, 1956). Whether the symbol is seen as being the same as what it indicates or whether it points beyond, to representation, is what distinguishes the apparent gift of the schizophrenic to understand symbolic thought.

For the schizophrenic, there is a symbolic equation underlying his very concrete thought. He actually has great difficulty in differentiating between the real object and its symbolic representation, as did the primitives who believed that they could have mastery over the elemental forces of the world by manipulating a symbolic representation of them (Modell, 1968, Chap. 1). For example, paleolithic cave art functioned as a creative illusion, "an illusion that provides for the participant a sense, through symbolic representation, of mastery, a mastery of the elemental forces of life and death..." (p. 16). In magical thought, the symbol is the object: "Symbol and object are inextricably fused—they represent an inseparable unity" (p. 19).

For the present purpose, it is important to see that it is within the vicissitudes of relationship to another person that a child becomes able to move from the level of magical, omnipotent denial of separateness to the acceptance of reality and the pain that objects (persons) can be lost. Modell develops this transition from the magical interconnection of one's private hallucinatory world and reality to the acceptance of the possibility of loss:

> The problem of the acceptance of painful reality can then be reduced to the problem of accepting the separateness of objects—that they can be lost. For...the fundamental aim of magical thinking is to create the illusion that the symbol and the object symbolized are inseparable....It is the central theme of this monograph that the acceptance of painful reality rests upon the same ego structures that permit the acceptance of the separateness of objects (p. 88).

Modell makes a convincing argument from this point for the unity between the creation of a cultural form and the creation of the image of a loved object, both involving the "interpenetration of the private vision with the public, conventionalized schemata: that is, *the modes of loving and knowing are inseparable*" (p. 165). [Italics mine.]

The connection between symbolic expression and human relatedness is further supported, most vividly, in the work of M. A. Sechehaye in the now famous cure of a "hopeless" case of schizophrenia through a method that she termed "symbolic realization." Her account is a particularly enlightening treatment of the use of symbols, since we are able to see the progression of the patient's grasp on reality from a severely regressed, autistic stage, to a gradual deliverance from the schizophrenic illness. At first Mme Sechehaye could make contact with the patient only through symbols that corresponded to the patient's undifferentiated state: the girl could respond only to "green apples," since they were "still attached to the tree," i.e., undifferentiated.

As treatment progressed, the patient could appropriate the reality of her mother-analyst's care through symbols of external reality, for example, a balloon, which symbolized the maternal breast, and a little doll, Moses, which was a symbol of the child's ego in reality. It was the testimony of the cured patient herself, who never returned to her schizophrenic state, that it was the symbols that had made contact with her. She expressed the view that had the analyst hit on the symbolic method sooner, it would have taken much less time to rescue her from psychosis.

In my own psychoanalytic work with children, I have had repeated confirmation of the connection between the ability to use symbols and the progressive response to personal encounter with the therapist. In two autistic children, whose play was mimetic and concrete over a period of weeks, there emerged sudden breakthroughs into new levels of play, where there was unmistakable projection—for the first time—of inner fantasy onto an outer object.

With one of these children, it was a large inflatable beach ball to which the child ran with a gasp of joy; he buried his face in it over and over, then found the small tube by which the ball was inflated, and sucked, and sucked, and sucked. With another, it was a piece of fur cloth that the child wrapped himself in, over and over, covering at last his face, his head, his entire body, that seemed to be a symbol to him.

When he wrapped himself, so that he was completely covered, he would call to me, "Wake me up! Wake me up!" I wondered whether the self-enclosure represented for him his isolation from others, and whether the cry to be waked was his yearning to be called out of his nearly autistic state. He would play this game over and over, and it seemed to me that he was dramatizing a journey from separation to relationship, through the medium of a symbol.

If we think back to the children introduced in Chapter I, it was William who demonstrated most clearly the beginnings of the use of symbol in connection with a personal encounter. The dough, the cake, the stories, and the other metaphors of nourishment, enabled him to participate in something vital in the containing relationship in such a way as to spark his own creative urge. A capacity, which had not appeared before, to use the toys and the images in the stories as expressions of new things happening in himself followed the connection with the symbolic nourishment.

It is striking that of the three children, William was the one who had had the least opportunity for human relationship; neither his mother nor his father was able to be accessible to him. His responsiveness to a new object relationship, concomitant with his making use of symbols, would seem to confirm the hypothesis that the use of symbol is a relational matter.

In concluding this inquiry into how and why children begin to use symbols, I want to point out that not only do the beginnings of symbolic thought and the beginnings of human relatedness coincide, but that the development of both also coincide. Rodrigué, whose work was mentioned above, spoke of the widening and deepening of the relatedness of his young patient in correspondence to his use of symbols:

> I consider that symbols enable the subject to conceive and elaborate his feelings and ideas concerning his objects. Each representational symbol embodies a conception of it. By means of the multiple symbolic forms a given object can take, the subject can work over and experience all the range of emotions related to his primary objects (p. 157).

> Symbol formation and symbol-using are not only indispensable to start intellectual and emotional development, but symbolization is fully active throughout life, underlying the increasingly sophisticated operations of adult thought (p. 153).

Winnicott saw the extension of the first symbolic experience widening into ever richer meaning of existence:

> No longer are we either introvert or extrovert. We experience life in the area of transitional phenomena, in the exciting interweave of subjectivity and objective observation, and in an area that is intermediate between the inner reality of the individual and the shared reality of the world that is external to individuals (1971, p. 64).

Rycroft, mentioned above, contributes further to the developmental aspect of the symbol:

> If used by the secondary process the symbol remains related to the outside world and symbol formation leads to the widening of the individual's libidinal interests. The fact that symbol-formation is a process capable of indefinite repetition...leads to the possibility of an ever-increasing extension of the individual's outer world: to his being able to find satisfaction in objects and activities increasingly remote from his primary instinctual interests. This is the process referred to by Jones in his description of 'civilization as a never-ending series of symbolic substitutions' (p. 144).[2]

As the thought of these various authors, representing different theoretical schools, seems to support the working hypothesis that children begin to use symbols in connection with people, and grow into richer interchange with the world around them through symbols, some light has been cast on the questions raised at the end of Chapter I. The children's journeys, so rich with symbolic creativity, and so marked by growth and personal discovery of what had been latent and unrealized, had something to do with their appropriation of human encounter. There is some mystery here that may come to further light as we proceed.

---

[2] This quotation from Jones would seem to be at variance with the restricted use of symbolism to which he adhered in the 1916 article mentioned above. Freud's theory of sublimation also transcended the narrow view of symbolism as retrogressive.

Chapter IV

THE RELATIONAL CONTEXT: CENTRALITY OF OBJECT RELATIONS IN PERSONALITY FORMATION AND SUBLIMATION

In the last chapter, the focus was on the beginnings and development of the child's use of symbol. I will turn now to the other side of the question raised at the end of Chapter I—how the symbol and the relationship are related to the personality changes in the children—, and explore in some detail the nature of human relationship as the matrix in which children become what they potentially are.

In recent decades, there has come increasingly to the fore in psychoanalytic thought an emphasis on the significance of human relationship in the development of the personality from the beginning, as well as in the capacity for sublimation specifically. It will be the purpose of the present chapter to explore this emphasis on the centrality of relationship in emotional development and sublimation. Chapter V will focus especially on the earliest human environment of infants, the qualities of what Winnicott calls "the holding environment" provided by the parents, which facilitates the unfolding of the nascent ego of the child and fosters creative living. It is the assumption here that the parental relationship serves as the paradigm for the therapeutic relationship, and that the illumination of the former will shed light also on the latter.[1]

The significance of human relationship in personality development was already explicit in Freud: His statement that the ego takes into itself "precipitates...of former object-cathexes" (1933b, p. 77) brings us squarely to face the idea that personality is a relational matter.

One has only briefly to come into contact with children whose early lives have been nearly devoid of personal give and take with other people in order to comprehend the profundity of this statement of Freud's. Since the effects on children of insufficient early relationships will be discussed later, I will only mention, in order to emphasize Freud's statement, that children who have had no effective parent figure in their lives have, among other deficits, a hole in the personality where the inner authority over one's actions is supposed to be, namely the place of the internalized parent in more fortunate children. They are like empty vessels that are waiting to be filled, and indeed these children seem to be able to attend to little else besides the pursuit of some belated satisfaction, some reparation for the hole left by the parent who was not there or could not be appropriated. Without intervention, they will spend a life-time of difficulty in living, trying to make of every potential relationship another mother of whom the old debt is demanded (Levy, 1937).

While Freud addressed the issue of object relations[2] primarily from the perspective of familial interrelationship at the time when the child becomes involved in the triangular dynamics of the oedipal stage of development, later psychoanalysts have focused on the importance of what happens in the very earliest relationship, namely in the tie of the infant with the mother.[3] It is generally acknowledged in the literature

---

[1] For an interesting discussion of the varying opinions regarding whether the psychoanalytic therapy situation is or is not a recapitulation of the early mother-child situation, see Modell, A. H. (1976).

[2] The term "object relations" as referring to interpersonal relationships of a significant nature is unfortunate language, but it is so well established in the literature that it is now virtually a technical term, and it will be employed as such in this paper.

[3] The term "mother" will be used throughout this paper to denote the nurturing figure who represents the mothering role to the infant. It could presumably refer to a father who has taken the role, or a grandparent, or some other surrogate. This statement does not assume that there would be no differences in the care afforded the infant under such circumstances, however.

that Freud took for granted an adequacy in the maternal nurture. In using the term "infant," for example (1911, p. 220n), he inserted as a parenthesis, the words "provided one includes with it the care it receives from its mother" (Winnicott, 1960, p. 39).

Since Freud made that rather off-hand comment, increasing attention has been paid to the developmental era to which it referred, namely the early mother-infant dyad, and an entire body of theoretical and clinical writing has stressed the significance of this dyad in personality formation and in psychopathology. While object relations was of course central in Freud's own thought, especially in the later structural theory, i.e., the way in which he understood the super-ego to come into being, as well as his insight into the dynamics of melancholia (1923, 1917c), it has been his successors who have pushed the significance of objects in emotional growth earlier than the oedipal and pre-oedipal stages and to a position of greater and greater consequence in personality development.

One school of thought, under the leadership of W. R. D. Fairbairn in England, and perhaps most familiar in this country through the work of Harry Guntrip, has gone so far as virtually to eliminate the theory of instincts as essential to understanding personality and to theorize that emotional development and psychopathology can be approached most fruitfully from the standpoint of object relations, or the position that it is in the media of personal relationship that the individual is shaped:

> I will...observe here that psychoanalytic theory today centers less and less on the control of instinct and more and more on the development of a stable core of selfhood—that is, the laying of the foundation of a strong personal ego in a good mother-infant relationship at the start of life, and its subsequent fate in the ever varying types of personal relationships, good and bad, that make up our life (Guntrip, 1971, p. 12f.).

The Object Relations school, which has made a growing impact on current psychoanalytic thought, has, according to Guntrip, made an effort to discard Freud's "psychobiology" and aim toward a psychodynamic science shorn of its ties to the physical-science thought forms to which Freud wanted to remain committed. "Object-relational thinking is the emancipation of the core of psychodynamic insight" (Guntrip, 1971, p. 33). For example, in this view, both sex and aggression are considered to be the dynamic reactions of a person-ego in and to an object-relational situation rather than instincts as such. Guntrip, following Fairbairn, largely rejects the idea of instincts, "which are not entities, and certainly not forces invading the ego from outside itself, giving it a kick in the pants" (Guntrip, 1971, p. 34).

In Object Relations theory, sex is treated as an "appetite," along with bodily needs like hunger, thirst, and the need for oxygen, sleep, and physical exercise. Aggression is understood to be a "personal defensive reaction against a threat to the ego" (Guntrip, 1971, p. 38). In effect, this school of thought necessarily equates intrapsychic dynamics with objects, bad and good, which to varying degrees of realism reflect the actual interaction with persons in the immediate human environment.

While I have not been convinced that interaction with objects can explain adequately the entire gamut of psychodynamic phenomena, I am indebted to these thinkers for drawing my attention to writers who have enriched and clarified my understanding of the significance of relationship in personality development and in sublimation, and for the ways in which these writers have informed my thinking in regard to Amy, John, and William. Among these are H. S. Sullivan and Melanie Klein.

Harry Stack Sullivan: His Interpersonal Theory

Sullivan was among the first to suggest that it is the interaction with "significant others"—as distinguished from instincts—that sheds the most light on personality development (Sullivan, 1953, 1965). In what has been called his own quaint way of describing what goes on in the human mind and what goes on between people, he developed a genre of ego-object relations theory, one might say, though his word for it was the "self-system." The self-system, or self-dynamism, Sullivan understood to be born "practically exclusively" out of the pursuit of security and satisfaction with "significant others." He saw the entire repertoire that one develops in order to deal with life—the vast system of operations, precautions, and awarenesses that are organized early in life and become patterned over time—as coming into being in connection with this pursuit of satisfaction and security in connection with the earliest important people in one's life.

The self develops, in his view, in connection with avoiding anxiety in the course of dealing with these significant persons, the anxiety meaning, in his terms, very simply the anticipation of disapproval of these significant others, or of their representations in the mind. That is to say, the significant other may be actually present in the form of a real person, or present in effect: significant others may be present only through "parataxic thinking," i.e., thinking that distorts reality by personal, autistic connections and associations; they may be, rather than actual persons, "personifications" of experiences in the past that are still dominating one's perceptions of new situations.

By "personifications" Sullivan means a mental construct of previous experience that attaches itself to other people and situations. For example, the personification of "mother" is not the same thing as the actual mother, but rather a derivative of experience with the "good nipple" and the "bad nipple." The good nipple is the personification of handling that has communicated tenderness to the child and successfully resolved the tension of certain needs. The bad nipple is the personification of handling that involved anxiety, or what he terms the "counter-vector" to the satisfaction or resolution of the tensions of certain needs.

These earliest personifications of "mother" become the core of the later personifications of the self: "good me" is thus the part of me that derives from patterned experiences of need-satisfying tenderness; "bad me" is derivative from patterned experiences of moderately anxiety-producing situations; and "not-me," that part of the self of which one is not aware, is born out of the "blow-on-the-head" kind of anxiety, i.e., the severe kind, which has involved in one's dealings with others an uncanny emotion, loathing, awe, or dread (Sullivan, 1953, p. 163).

Thus, in Sullivan's system, which came out of his own acute clinical observations, it is in the very first relationship, i.e., with the mothering one, that the infant begins to shape perceptions and actions in accordance with certain signs read in the mother—for example, certain mild signs of worry, displeasure or anxiety in the mother's face and manner—that is, according to the diminishing or increasing of anxiety in this first interpersonal situation, very much as the amoeba learns to alter its direction as it approaches hot water. In the infancy setting, Sullivan applies this idea to the interactions at the oral and anal zones, where the system of precautions, alertnesses, symbols, and signs of warning come into play in the interpersonal occurrences connected to the handling of these zonal needs. It is here that the infant learns to chart a course around the "hot and cold water," that is, the anxiety or euphoria (tenderness imparting) in the interaction that is imparted to the infant "empathically" by the mother.

Object relations and their significance in personality formations have thus come to the fore in the unique vocabulary and simple operational concepts of Sullivan. His focus in psychiatric theory might have the implication that the changes we saw in Amy, John, and William were somehow related to the interpersonal connection with the therapist. Those new houses and wider avenues and stronger swords were not, from the perspective of Sullivan, entirely private creations explicable solely in terms of intrapsychic shifts. The "not-me," and the "bad me" in each child shrank in proportion to the "me," and the "good me," and it involved "significant others" in some way that may come to further light.

Melanie Klein

The Object Relations school, mentioned above, in spite of major disagreement with Melanie Klein (Kernberg, 1969), has identified her work as the turning point from a mechanistic psychoanalytic theory to a personal one. Harry Guntrip (1969, 1971) attributes to her a new conception of endopsychic structure: from instincts to an inner world of personal object relations:

> *After Klein, it became possible to see the human psyche as an internal world of a fully personal nature, a world of internalized ego-object relationships, which partly realistically and partly in highly distorted ways reproduced the ego's relationships to personal objects in the real outer world* (1969, p. 407). [Entire passage his italics.]

Klein's theory of personality development has elicited controversy in many quarters (Roazen, 1975, p. 485f.), but few question the impact of her work on the deepened understanding of how it is that personality is shaped in the media of human relationship. Her emphasis is sounded clearly in the following statement:

The analysis of very young children has taught me that there is no instinctual urge, no anxiety situation, no mental process which does not involve objects, external or internal; in other words, object-relations are at the *centre* of emotional life (Klein, 1952b, p. 53). [Italics hers.]

For the present task, that of investigating human relationship as the matrix in which children can become whole, Klein's work is particularly useful in three aspects: 1) The centrality of objects in the personality as a whole, 2) Emotional development as schematized around relationships with objects as paramount over libidinal zones, and 3) Symbol formation and sublimation specifically as intimately connected with experience with objects from the very beginning.

Centrality of Objects in Personality

It was stated above that in the Object Relations school there appears to be a nearly synonymous meaning given to intrapsychic dynamics and object relations, according to my reading of their work (i.e., Guntrip, 1971). It would be an error to attribute that reductionism to Melanie Klein. For her, the inner world involves from the beginning an unconscious struggle between forces of life and death, of creativity and destructiveness, of love and hate. In this regard, there are similarities in her thinking not only to the thought of Freud in regard to life and death instincts, but also to the thought of Jung, namely that there are forces operating on the psyche that cannot be understood as mere reactions of an ego to the external world.

However, it is fair to say that in her view the human psyche certainly cannot be understood apart from its matrix of personal relatedness, in the context of which the inner and outer world are inextricably intermeshed by processes, largely unconscious, which she delineates. The "outer world" means fundamentally significant other persons in one's life, and the "inner world" is made up of one's own instincts interwoven with fantasies around "good" objects and "bad" objects. These good and bad objects are internal representations of real objects, that is, persons perceived through the medium of a certain kind of lens, i.e., a lens highly colored by projection and introjection.

These good objects and bad objects are of course not unrelated to the parental handling, but they are composites of the child's own instinctual conflicts, as well as the highly personalized, emotionally charged perceptions of the real objects involved in the care of the child, and, not incidentally, the derivatives of the forces of life and death, which, according to Klein, rage in the infant from the beginning.[4] Thus, in Klein's view, the foundations of personality are to be understood in the context of this constant interchange between two worlds, the outer and the inner, between which there is constant traffic through the processes of introjection and projection, and which are never completely sorted out from each other. That both of these worlds are peopled, that is, that objects, real and distorted by various forces, make up their intrinsic nature is the point of emphasis here.

It is clear that these developments begin in the very first relationship, that with the mother, and, for Klein, even more specifically with the breast.[5] The ego comes into being, in her view, in connection with this first object:

> As I see it, object relations start almost at birth. The mother in her good aspects—loving, helping, feeding the child—is the first good object that the infant makes a part of his inner world....If the mother is taken into the child's inner world as a good and dependable object, an element of strength is added to the ego. For I assume that the ego develops largely around this good object, and the identification with the good characteristics of the mother becomes the basis for further helpful identifications (Klein, 1959, p. 251).

Klein's specific emphasis on the breast as the first object is shown here in this passage:

> The breast, on which the life and death instincts are projected, is the first object which by introjection is internalized. In this way both instincts find an object to which they attach themselves and thereby by projection and re-introjection the ego is enriched as well as strengthened (1958, p. 245).

These words introduce Klein's thought that the roots of love and hate are to be found in the experience with the breast, in that both good

---

[4] It is Klein's adherence to the idea of life and death instincts that is not acceptable to Object Relations theorists (Kernberg, 1969; Guntrip, 1971), as well as to many other psychoanalytic writers.

[5] Klein extends the use of the word "breast" to the feeding with a bottle by the mothering person (1952a, p. 99) "if there is close physical nearness to the mother and the infant is handled and fed in a loving way." However, she distinguishes between the two experiences. For a discussion of this issue, see footnote on p. 117 of *Envy and Gratitude*.

The Relational Context: Centrality of Object Relations   77

feelings and bad feelings, i.e., both poles of experience, begin in connection with gratification and frustration by this object:

> In the earliest stages, love and understanding are expressed through the mother's handling of her baby, and lead to a certain unconscious oneness that is based on the unconscious of the mother and of the child being in close relation to each other. The infant's resultant feeling of being understood underlies the first and fundamental relation in his life—the relation to the mother. At the same time, frustration, discomfort and pain, which I suggested are experienced as persecution, enter as well into his feelings about his mother, because in the first few months she represents to the child the whole of the external world; therefore both good and bad come into his mind from her, and this leads to a twofold attitude toward the mother even under the best possible conditions (1959, p. 248).

That the child experiences frustration as persecutory is discussed this way:

> This can be explained by the fact that the young infant, without being able to grasp it intellectually, feels unconsciously every discomfort as though it were inflicted on him by hostile forces (1959, p. 248).

Adrian Stokes, a British philosopher of art, who was analyzed by Klein and whose work is much enriched by her insights, enlarged on this idea that frustration at the breast is experienced as persecutory:

> I have in mind...a feeling of emptiness or absence that, upon projection, enormously aggravates the deprivations of hunger and thus endows the frustrating breast with a virulent badness or power of persecution. It seems to me that to posit a projection of a sense of absence stimulated by the pull of death, in association with hunger, clarifies the incidence as well as the huge power of persecutory anxiety: it means that two kinds coincide, the psychological sense of absence and a somatic absence (Stokes, 1973a, p. 64).

Thus the centrality of object relations in Klein's work is seen first in the way in which the mothering one serves as the original ego nucleus of the infant (1957, p. 179f.); by being present in such a way that both loving and destructive feelings may be experienced and sorted out in connection with her, the mother is at the core of the formation and the enrichment of the child's ego.[6]

Schema of Emotional Development as Object-Centered

Klein did not abandon the Freudian theory of psychosocial development based on successive stages of libidinal organization centered in different bodily zones; however, in effect, these concepts have been overshadowed by her emphasis on personality growth as a matter of changes in specific configurations of anxieties, defenses, and feelings *in regard to the primary relationship*, especially the way in which loving feelings and destructive feelings are handled at different phases of early development.

To put the matter in very simple terms, one might say that she observed and stated that an infant in the early months, given adequate opportunity through the mothering one, goes through two different normal stages in regard to the handling of the "good" and the "bad." The more primitive way of handling or sorting out the bad, which, as explained above, derives from the inevitable frustrations and discomforts of infancy as these are commingled with the child's own instincts and exaggerated by innate forces, is to "split" the bad from the good and to experience the bad as coming at one, rather than being in one.

Because the basic process here is projection, Klein uses the somewhat misleading term of "paranoid-schizoid position" to encapsulate this more primitive way in which the two poles of experience, the bad and the good, are handled. The introjection of the good and the projection of the bad is primary; however, this dynamic can also work in the opposite way: the good can be projected in order to protect it from the bad, and the bad can be introjected in order to control it or identify with it. It is important to recognize that this arrangement is a normal one, according to Klein, and the terminology is not meant to imply that there is necessarily a psychopathology involved. In fact, this splitting, and the various combinations of introjections and

---

[6] Klein's views on these matters are to be found throughout the two volumes of her collected papers, *Love, Guilt and Reparation*, and *Envy and Gratitude*, as well as in *The Psycho-Analysis of Children*, and *Narrative of a Child Analysis*. For a thorough and readable presentation of her work, see Hanna Segal, *Introduction to the Work of Melanie Klein* (1964).

projections, is useful in that it enables infants to begin to sort out their perceptions of the bad and the good and paves the way for later more integrative processes.

Hanna Segal, a Kleinian analyst who has performed the valuable service of presenting Klein's views in a very clear and systematic way (1964), explains the usefulness of this emotional development:

> I have emphasized...that, in normal development, the paranoid-schizoid position is characterized by a split between the good and the bad objects and the loving and hating ego, a split in which good experiences predominate over bad ones. This is a necessary pre-condition for integration in later stages of development. I have also emphasized that, at this stage, the infant comes to organize his perceptions by means of projective and introjective processes (Segal, 1964, p. 42).

From this initial way of organizing experience by the dividing up of good and bad and by a somewhat constant shuffling and counterchange between the inner world and the outer world, the infant, given adequate opportunity for experience under conditions that are favorable to growth (Chapter V), will make a definitive advance to a second stage in the organization of the feelings and anxieties that have come into play in connection with the mother.

The achievement of this second stage of development, which Klein sees as decisive for the individual's capacity to form and sustain mutual human relationships throughout life, is also significant enough to be called a "position." That is, it is a milestone at which one arrives if the encounter in the first relationship has made possible the predominance of the good inside over the bad inside in such a way that the necessity for projection and "splitting" is lessened.

While the configurations of feelings and unconscious processes of anxiety and defense are quite complex in this formulation of Klein's, the most significant aspect of this second stage of emotional development can be said to be the major shift in the infant's handling of ambivalence: namely, that the bad as well as the good begin to be sensed as emanating from one person, namely the mother, and therefore the *internalized* mother—seen above to be the ego nucleus of the infant—is experienced as both good and bad.

In other words, the integration of the fairy godmother and the bad witch, to use the fairy-tale terms, has begun to take place. Since both the fairy godmother and the bad witch are internal to every child as a result of the colored lenses, composed of the child's own given ambivalence, to some extent, through which the parental care is perceived, there is a corresponding coalescence of good and bad in the ego.

In effect, this development means that no longer is "persecutory anxiety," or the experience of having all the bad coming at one, the central threat to the ego. A new configuration of matters has now come about so that threat of annihilation of the ego by bad forces is replaced by another, perhaps equally distressing, fear: the new fear is that the bad, destructive impulses, now perceived to be inside the ego as well as outside, will destroy, or perhaps have already destroyed, the good object and the good feelings inside.

Because the principal anxiety here is the fear of losing—through one's own destructive impulse—the good object, on whom the infant depends for all life-giving sustenance, and which is synonymous with the core of the ego, Klein called this phase the "depressive position." Again, as in the case of "paranoid-schizoid," the wording seems to be unfortunate, since the term "depressive" is so strongly associated with psychopathology.

It needs to be stressed again that the issue here is stages of normal development, and indeed emotional achievement, as distinguished from an illness of mood. The use of the word "depressive" is no doubt connected with the emphasis at this stage on feelings of mourning and guilt, new feelings experienced by the infant as a result of sensing impulses within that have, or will have, devoured and destroyed the good internal object, causing good feelings to be overcome by bad ones. But in terms of emotional growth, the development is a highly favorable one, and one on which hangs the capacity for all genuine human relationship.

Winnicott, who considered that Klein's insight into this emotional configuration at the "depressive" position was her most lasting contribution (Winnicott, 1962, p. 176), clarified that the momentous achievement here is the advance from "ruthlessness" to "ruth" (concern) in mental life (Winnicott, 1954, 1958, 1962). In the context of an adequate holding environment, a concept that will be elaborated in the next chapter, the infant is enabled to arrive at a position of concern deriving from the owning of one's destructive impulses and the urge to make reparation for the "hole" that one has made (1954, p. 262f).

The Relational Context: Centrality of Object Relations 81

The import of this way of looking at emotional development could easily be underestimated. What is being addressed here is the source, from one point of view, of all ethical responsibility, namely the capacity to care about, and to feel responsible for, the effects of one's feelings and actions—and the effects of one's instincts—on other human beings. As the word "guilt," since Freud, has been associated so frequently with a psychopathology of guilt, i.e., neurotic guilt, it is important to emphasize in the present connection that the ability to feel inner compunction is an emotional achievement, and an achievement of decisive consequence in the flowering of a child into the human community. Indeed, one might say that without the ability to feel uneasiness of conscience, regret over giving pain to another, to mind or care when another feels hurt, to feel contrition over wrongdoing—from the "guilt" side—, and to feel responsible and involved enough to want to make things right, to repair, to make restitution—the "concern" side of the matter—, one is not yet quite fully human.

The absence of this achievement of caring results in an indifference to others and an emotional deadness, which in the current literature is called "disease of non-attachment," and it may well be that this disease may in our time prove to be more lethal in social living than classical neurosis. Selma Fraiberg, a child analyst who has contributed greatly to our understanding of the needs of children, writes of this disease of non-attachment, and her picture of those who are unattached to others by any sense of caring is very moving:

> The narrative of their lives reads like a vagrant journey with chance encounters and transient partnerships. Since no partner is valued, any one partner can be exchanged for any other; in the absence of love, there is no pain in loss. Indeed, the other striking characteristic of such people is their impoverished emotional range. There is no joy, no grief, no guilt, and no remorse. In the absence of human ties, a conscience cannot be formed; even the qualities of self-observation and self-criticism fail to develop....
>
> A good many of these hollow men remain anonymous in our society. But there are conditions under which they rise from anonymity and confront us with dead, unsmiling faces....The deadness within demands at times powerful psychic jolts in order to affirm existence. Some get their jolts from drugs. Others are driven to perform brutal acts....Victims of such acts are chosen indiscriminately and anonymously. There is no motive, as such, because the man who has no human connections does not have specific objects for his hatred....There is no remorse, often no self-defense...(1977, p. 47f.).

When one is thus confronted with a picture of what the human condition reveals in the absence of the capacity to *care*, and the absence of any capacity for the gladness of restitution, the weight of Klein's contribution in her developmental schema comes more clearly into focus.

It is also evident from Fraiberg's writing that the significance of the earliest object relationship in providing the matrix for this achievement of caring cannot be overlooked. Seen from Klein's viewpoint, it is this first relationship, in which the depressive position is either worked through or not worked through, that is decisive for the way in which one's relationships with others are lived out. Whether one is stuck with the persecutory experience of badness and destructiveness, always perceiving it to come from the outside toward one, or whether one can shoulder one's own ambivalence—can experience concern and guilt over one's own destructiveness, can feel joy in restitution, and can feel deeply and empathically the emotional position of others in his life—is staked out right here in the first relationship.

It is important to add that neither Klein nor Winnicott is so pessimistic as to believe that this early success or failure at the depressive position is unalterable or that it is a matter of all or nothing. All of us, apparently, go through life with some mixture of these two ways of handling ambivalence, and, furthermore, there is always a possibility of a corrective relational experience that may modify the nature of the internal objects that have served as the retainers of the early experience. In Klein's view, for example, alteration of the internal objects is the primary work of psychoanalytic therapy:

> In the course of treatment, the psycho-analyst comes to represent in the transference situation a variety of figures corresponding to those which were introjected in early development....He is, therefore, at times introjected as a persecutory, at other times as an ideal figure, with all shades and degrees in between.

> As persecutory and depressive anxieties are experienced and ultimately reduced during analysis, a greater synthesis between the various aspects of the analyst comes about together with a greater synthesis between the various aspects of the super-ego. In other words, the earliest frightening figures undergo an essential alteration in the patient's mind—one might say that they basically improve. Good objects—as distinct from idealized ones—can be securely established in the mind only if the strong split

between persecutory and ideal figures has diminished, if aggressive and libidinal impulses have come closer together and hatred has been mitigated by love (1950, p. 47).

However, the emphasis in the present discussion is that Klein's theory stresses that personality structure is essentially laid down by the way in which object relations are integrated in the earliest relational matrix (Segal, 1964, p. xiii).

While Klein's view that emotional development can be understood in terms of the "paranoid-schizoid" and "depressive" positions was initially elusive and unconvincing to me, the theory has come to life in my experience with children in clinical work. For example, in considering the changes in William, the third child we met in Chapter I, is not this change in "positions" one way to look at them? He moved from his basic stance of "hitting people in the face," without regret, to a way of being with me and with his teachers and the other children that was characterized by the capacity to feel affection, to suffer grief—with real tears—, and by the kind of human attachment that could move him to write a letter of reconciliation:

> I am happy. Is about time I'm happy....Cause I feel better, feel happy now I'm not mad at Dorothy. I hope she feel happy cause I'm not mad at Dorothy no more.

Perhaps one can say that William moved from the position of "ruthlessness" to "ruth" in the experience of a new object relationship.

Other children come to mind also, in fact, dozens of children who have come to me in various states of ruthlessness, and it cannot be coincidence that not one of these children had enjoyed what Fraiberg calls "every child's birthright," namely an opportunity to begin life within the security of a nurturing bond with the mother. Some of these children advanced to the ability to care and to want to make restitution more decisively that others, but for all of them it could be said that the growth of a capacity to feel guilt and responsibility for their urges and actions—to feel concern for another—was the primary task at hand, and, to the degree that this task was accomplished, it was through the intervention of a new kind of maternal relationship.

Of particular interest, in connection with Klein's theory, is that with more than one of these children, a great deal of the therapy centered around the extreme destructiveness experienced in the context of a "good feed," symbolically speaking.

For example, a particularly assaultive young fellow of nine years proceeded in a most unusual way in his psychotherapy:

When this child was first assigned to me, in the clinic school where William was my patient also, he was quite frightened at the notion of spending time with me in a playroom. He was very aloof and would run in the other direction when I went to his classroom to invite him for his session. Very gradually, as I was able to communicate to him that there were no strings on the invitation, that is, that I would be there for him whether or not he wished to come—that "the time was his and no one else could have it"—he thawed a bit and decided he would give the situation a try. The "try" was quite circumscribed, in that for some weeks he would agree at the outset to stay for "two minutes." I agreed on the terms, and for two minutes—gradually extended by him to five, then ten, then at last a half-hour—the child would engage in one game of his own invention. He would toss a ball into a box and give me explicit instructions as to what I was to say: if the ball went into the box, I was to say "yea-a—a," and, if the ball did not go into the box, I was to say "boo—oo—oo."

I carried out my part in a satisfactory way, apparently, because at the end of three or four months of this unique approach to psychotherapy, he introduced something new. He asked me if we might have tea, with sugar. In addition, he became interested in the flour-and-salt dough, with which William also made his way forward. The format for the sessions, from this time until the child was considered by all of us at the school to be ready to leave us, was always the same: 1) he would ask to make the dough, which he took away with him in two round lumps, and 2) he would make tea, which he sugared prodigiously. Sometimes he altered the order of these two activities, that is, he would make tea first and then make dough.

The child initiated, from time to time, conversation about what was going on in his life, but the significant happenings of the therapy took place around this "good feed." Sometimes he would show me his arm muscle and explain how strong he was getting "because of the tea," and once he was moved to a spontaneous expression of gratitude, bowed his head and uttered a kind of prayer of thanks "for the tea and for nice people."[7]

At other times, something else occurred: quite unpredictably, this child would interrupt his play and go into a nearly uncontrollable rage. Until I could physically restrain him, he would attempt to hit, kick, curse, and even bite me, hurling at me unquotable epithets and accusations. The good feelings he had had moments earlier were now replaced by violent hatred and destructive urges, and it required all of my resources successfully to restrain him, terminate the session, and get him back to class in some measure of control.

At these times, I felt my main therapeutic task, in addition to supplying the missing controls, was to survive the destructive attacks without counter-aggression and without being destroyed as a good object for the child.[8] Each time, I made a point to seek the child out several hours later, ask whether he was feeling better, let him know that he certainly had gotten out of control, and that he certainly had made me angry, but that I still liked him, and I would see him at our next session. The child would respond by heaving a large sigh of relief and by giving me a wide grin of unmistakable joy. At the next session he would tell me how sorry he was for what he had done, and then he would make tea and make dough.

I tell this story because I think this child moved from a position of "ruthlessness" to a position of concern. In time, his outbursts of rage ceased, and it seemed that the good inside had come to predominate over the bad, a development that made it less necessary to project the bad onto the therapist and then to attack it "out there." He learned to feel genuinely sorry and to feel guilt "for the hole he had made," to use Winnicott's phrase; he, along with William, learned to cry, with tears, when he felt disappointed or hurt, as, for example, when he learned that he would be going to a new school and leaving his teacher, his friends, and his therapist.

Further, he came to feel, in the aftermath of anger and destructiveness, the *urge to make reparation*. I underline these words for emphasis,

---

[7] Klein's "Envy and Gratitude" (1957) very much enriched my thinking about this incident.

[8] My experience corresponds with Winnicott's emphasis on the importance of the "survival" of the mother (or therapist) of the destructive rage of the child (or patient) (1954, p. 267f.).

because they bring us, in the discussion of Klein, to that part of her theory that addresses most directly the question being pursued here, namely the connection between a child's close relationships and his ability to sublimate his urges, that is, creatively to transform these urges into something else.

Symbol Formation and Sublimation in Klein's Theory: The Connection with Objects

In Klein's view, it is the advance to the stage she calls the "depressive position," discussed above, which gives rise, along with feelings of guilt and grief over the damage one has in fantasy done to the object, to sublimation, or an urge to make reparation and to recreate (in unconscious fantasy) the damaged object:

> The pain of mourning experienced in the depressive position, and the reparative drives developed to restore the loved internal objects, are the basis of creativity and sublimation. These reparative activities are directed toward both the object and the self. They are done partly in interest of self-preservation....The infant's longing to recreate his lost objects gives him the impulse to put together what has been torn asunder, to reconstruct what has been destroyed, to recreate and to create. At the same time, his wish to spare his objects leads him to sublimate his impulses when they are felt to be destructive. Thus, his concern for his object modifies his instinctual aims and brings about an inhibition of instinctual drives....
>
> At this point the genesis of symbol formation can be seen. In order to spare the object, the infant partly inhibits his instincts and partly displaces them onto substitutes—the beginning of symbol formation. The processes of sublimation and symbol formation are closely linked and are both the outcome of conflicts and anxieties pertaining to the depressive position (Segal, 1964, p. 62).

Segal thus gives us a very succinct introduction to Klein's view of symbol formation and sublimation. In an earlier article (1952, p. 196f.), Segal presented an interesting and persuasive argument for this view that it is the wish to restore and recreate objects associated with unconscious sadistic fantasies, and the guilt, grief, and fear accompanying these fantasies, which underlie sublimation and creativity. Basing her presentation on Proust, who maintained that an artist is compelled to create by his need to recover his lost past, she expressed the view that the urge to recreate, as well as to create, is present in the unconscious of all artists.[9] She summed up her thought this way:

> ...All creation is really a re-creation of a once loved and once whole, but now lost and ruined object, a ruined internal world and self. It is when the world within us is destroyed, when it is dead and loveless, when our loved ones are in fragments, and we ourselves in helpless despair—it is then that we must recreate our world anew, re-assemble the pieces, infuse life into dead fragments, re-create life (Segal, 1952, p. 199).

Because Klein's view of symbol formation and sublimation is so germane to the present inquiry into how the children's therapeutic journeys in Chapter I involve symbolic creativity in the context of relationship, I want to take a closer look at her thought about it.

As pointed out above, Klein asserted that it is in the first human contact, that with the mother's breast, that both the good feelings and the bad feelings of the infant come into play and form the basis for all later relationships. From this initial attachment, in her view, this original love and hate are then displaced to new objects and to new activities through symbolic substitution. Symbolic equation makes it possible for the fantasies and feelings that are first connected to the mother to become elaborated into wider interests:

> The process by which we displace love from the first people we cherish to other people is extended from earliest childhood onward to things. In this way we develop interests and activities into which we put some of the love that originally belonged to people. In the baby's mind, one part of the body can stand for another part, and an object for parts of the body or for people. In this symbolic way, any round object may, in the child's unconscious mind, come to stand for the mother's breast. By a gradual process, anything that is felt to give out goodness and beauty and that calls forth pleasure and satisfaction, in the physical or in a wider sense, can in the unconscious mind take the place of this ever-bountiful breast, and of the whole mother...(Klein, 1937, p. 333).

Klein's passage brings to mind William's dough, and his cake, and the use he was able to make of these supplies in the beginnings of his movement outward toward new interests and toward other people. They clearly connected, in the child's unconscious mind, with the

---

[9] For a most interesting and detailed account of an analysis of an artist that contributes rich clinical material in support of this view, see Heimann (1942).

bountiful breast, if Klein is right that anything that is felt to give out goodness and calls forth pleasure and satisfaction has this inner reference. It seems likely that the fantasies and feelings that became attached to the dough, which enabled him to experience the presence of the good mother, were then elaborated into wider interests, such as the stories, his symbolic play, and his learning tasks.

It is important to note that in Klein's view of sublimation, it is both the gratifying, good experience at the mother's breast and the frustrating, bad experience at the mother's breast that deeply affect the capacity for sublimation. So that, on the one hand, she says:

> I suggest that the happiness experienced in infancy and the love for the good object which enriches the personality underlie the capacity for enjoyment and sublimation and still make themselves felt in old age (Klein, 1957, p. 203).

On the other hand, it is the bad feelings experienced in connection with the mother that give rise to urges to repair the damage that in unconscious fantasy has been felt to destroy the good object, as pointed out above by Segal. In addition to this urge to make reparation, Klein observes that destructive impulses can serve as impetus and inspiration for creativity through their very unacceptableness:

> The more the ego can integrate its destructive impulses and synthesize its different aspects of its objects, the richer it becomes; for the split-off parts of the self and of impulses which are rejected because they arouse anxiety and give pain also contain valuable aspects of the personality and of the phantasy life which is impoverished by splitting them off. Though the rejected aspects of the self and of internalized objects contribute to instability, they are also at the source of inspiration in artistic productions and in various intellectual activities (Klein, 1958, p. 245).

Klein's comments above sound an appropriate word of caution that to stress either the positive or the negative experiences of living, to the exclusion of the other, in attempting to understand sublimation and creative activity is reductionistic. Examples of towering creative genius in persons who suffered disaster in personal life instruct us that sublimation is not to be understood simply as an outgrowth of benign parental relationship. On the other hand, the inability of children like William to sublimate their instinctual urges in the absence of a

The Relational Context: Centrality of Object Relations

nourishing relationship reminds us that there is another side to the matter: personal disaster as such does not necessarily lead to creativity.

In the therapeutic journeys, it seemed to be evident that it was the containing relationship that brought forth into an awakening of life parts of the self that had been split off. For example, Amy's caterpillars, the wriggly little creatures that at first were relegated to the isolated dog house, became transformed in time to dancing worms that frolicked joyfully around the room. They could sail through the air, and dance, and fly around. There was an explosion of boundaries, a kindling of creative urge, and a degree of freedom of expression that had been previously unavailable to the child.

It is clear from the work of Melanie Klein that the ego itself, the developmental stages by which the ego is enriched, and the ego's ability to transform and displace the early passions into creative interests through symbol formation—that is, the ability to sublimate instinctual drives—is developed largely around the introjected mother. The conclusion from her work brings us back to the same point emphasized in the exploration of the theories of Freud and Jung, and perhaps even more explicitly: namely, that symbol formation and the transformation of instinctual impulses cannot be divorced from the context of human relationship, and, very specifically, from the role of early mothering in its origins.

At several points in this discussion of the centrality of object relations in sublimation, I have mentioned that one of the requisites for the capacity to transform the instinctual energies creatively into new forms—as William and all other impulse-ridden children teach us—is the adequacy of the "holding" function of the mother during the early weeks and months of life. It will be the purpose of the next chapter to explore in some detail what is involved in this "holding," and what Winnicott called "the facilitating environment."

Chapter V

THE RELATIONAL CONTEXT: THE HOLDING ENVIRONMENT

D.W. Winnicott, having come to psychoanalysis by way of pediatrics, was able to observe the development of human personality from two points of advantage: his pediatric work with mothers and babies provided opportunity for learning a great deal about what goes on at the beginning of life, and his analytic work with patients who came to him because of emotional suffering later on provided insight from another viewpoint. Because he was in this unusual position to perceive the recapitulations of parent-infant phenomena in the transference relationship of psychoanalysis, he was especially qualified to contribute an exposition of Freud's parenthetical phrase, "...when one considers that the infant—provided one includes with it the care it receives from its mother—does almost realize a psychical system of this kind." That is to say, Winnicott was able to shed a great deal of light on that phrase from Freud (1911) and on the nature of maternal care (Winnicott, 1960, p. 39f.).

Winnicott emphasized that, in one sense, we cannot talk about "an infant," but must first speak about a dyad, the child-mother unit, at a time "when the infant has not separated out from the maternal care on which there exists absolute dependence in a psychological sense"

(1960, p. 38). He spelled out the characteristics of the environmental provision that is necessary at this time:

> It meets psychological needs. Here physiology and psychology have not yet become distinct, or are only in the process of doing so; and It is reliable. But the environmental provision is not mechanically reliable. It is reliable in a way that implies the mother's empathy.
> Holding:
>
>> Protects from physiological insult.
>>
>> Takes account of the infant's skin sensitivity—touch, temperature, auditory sensitivity, visual sensitivity, sensitivity to falling (action of gravity) and of the infant's lack of knowledge of the existence of anything other than the self.
>>
>> It includes the whole routine of care throughout the day and night, and it is not the same with any two infants because it is part of the infant, and no two infants are alike.
>>
>> Also it follows the minute day-to-day changes belonging to the infant's growth and development, both physical and psychological (1960, p. 48f.).

This maternal care, on a continuum with the prenatal state, is a silent, unnoticed-if-it-is-there provision of a nesting place, in which the nascent ego of the child begins to grow. In Winnicott's words, it makes possible the "continuity of being" of the child (1960, p. 54), and, when it fails, it subjects the child to extreme anxiety tantamount to "ego-weakening":

> As a result of success in maternal care there is built up in the infant a continuity of being which is the basis of ego-strength; whereas the result of each failure in maternal care is that the continuity of being is interrupted by reactions to the consequences of that failure, with resultant ego-weakening. Such interruptions constitute annihilation, and are evidently associated with pain of psychotic quality and intensity. In the extreme case the infant exists only on the basis of a continuity of reactions to impingement and of recoveries from such reactions. This is in great contrast to the continuity of being which is my conception of ego-strength (1969, p. 52).

Before exploring further some of the implications of the holding environment as understood by Winnicott for our understanding of the changes in Amy, John, and William, it may be useful to take a brief overview of other significant contributions in the literature regarding maternal care and the mother-child dyad as background for further investigation.

Bonding

There is now considerable evidence that an early "bonding" between mother and infant is indispensable for normal emotional development (Mahler and Pine, 1975; Klaus and Kennel, 1976; Fraiberg, 1977). In order to assess the strength of the attachment characteristic of this bond, some authors have termed it a "symbiosis" (Mahler, 1972, 1975; Searles, 1965), presumably with the implication that it is a union that is advantageous to both parties involved. The success of this early bonding is seen to be necessary for cognitive development (Dunn, 1977); for the ability to use toys and through them to cathect the larger world (Provence and Ritvo, 1961; Benedek, 1938; Greenacre, 1960; Klein, 1930); for ability to control and channel the drives (Fraiberg, 1977; Kris, 1955; Levy, 1937; Spitz, 1965); for the ability to form love ties and mutual relationship later in life (Fraiberg, 1977; Harlow, 1959, 1965; Levy, 1937; Spitz, 1965).

A strong scientific base for the now burgeoning literature on this early bond was provided by John Bowlby in his classic two-volume work on Attachment and Loss (1969, 1973). Dr. Bowlby analyzed thoroughly the nature of the child's tie to the mother, examined its roots, and formulated a theory as to how the tie begins and develops, what fosters it or hinders it, the role of this attachment in the personality development of the child, and the emotional and behavioral effects on the child of premature separation from the mothering bond. As confirmation of Bowlby's work, Dorothy Burlingham and Anna Freud (1942) reported on the broad range of emotional disturbance in British children who during the war were separated from the primary love tie.

René Spitz, a psychoanalyst who devoted much of his productive work to the study of the first year of life, described the infant-mother dyad as "an ego-ism of two," a relationship "insulated from the surround and held together by extraordinarily powerful affective bonds" (1965, p. 127). He stressed that the personality of the infant is shaped through a "continual reciprocal affective exchange" within the infant-mother dyad. It was his view that this affective interchange underlies and precedes all other psychic functions, and that all of these subsequent functions develop on the basis of this foundational bond (1965, p. 140; 1970, p. 42f.). He found that within this dyad there is a near "totality" of communication, analogous to the "coenesthetic" communication between animals, and which is present in primitive societies and in certain mystical and extra-sensory, "pre-diacritic" symbolic communications that have traces still in our society (1965, p. 134f.). This totality of communication is facilitated by a heightened sensitivity and awareness of a mother to her baby and also by the baby's perception of the mother's moods (1965, p. 127).

This heightened awareness and near-telepathic communication is similar to what Winnicott saw to derive from a "primary maternal preoccupation," through which a mother achieves a very powerful sense of what the baby needs (Winnicott, 1960, p. 53). Spitz emphasizes that the affective exchange in the dyad is to be understood as a cumulative experience, in which isolated traumatic events are rarely significant in comparison with the day to day accumulation of repeated sequences of affective communication:

> Affective signals generated by maternal moods seem to become a form of communication with the infant. These exchanges between mother and child go on uninterruptedly, without the mother necessarily being aware of them. This mode of communication between mother and child exerts a constant pressure which shapes the infantile psyche....I speak of "pressure" only because the words to convey these extraordinarily subtle and intangible exchanges have never been coined. I am trying to describe a process of which only the most superficial manifestations can be apprehended. Pressure and giving way alternate and combine to influence now one function, then another among which unfold with maturation, retarding some, facilitating others....Below this surface the ebb and flow of affective energies move the tides which channel the current of personality development into one direction or the other (Spitz, 1965, p. 138f.).

In addition to his contribution in regard to the nature of the mother-child bond, Spitz clarified the difference between what he called the "emotional deficiency" situation, wherein a child is deprived of the mothering presence, and the "psychotoxic situation," which refers to a disturbed affective climate between mother and child, as, for example, when a mother is depressed or otherwise severely "out of tune with her surround" (1965, p. 210f.).

Spitz' conclusions about the consequences of failure or absence of the mother-infant bond are indeed sobering. Reviewing the fate of those not given the opportunity to experience the mother-infant relationship, which he calls "the template for all later human relationship and social living" (1965, p. 296), he says:

> Such individuals will be unable to understand, much less discover and join the intricate and many-hued bonds of relations which they have never had. The relations they are able to form barely reach the level of identification and hardly go beyond, because they have never been able to achieve the earliest, the most elementary one, the anaclitic relation with their mother. The misery of these infants will be translated into the bleakness of the adolescent's social relations. Deprived of the affective nourishment to which they were entitled, their only resource is violence. The only path which remains open to them is the destruction of a social order of which they are the victims. Infants without love, they will end as adults full of hate (1965, p. 300).

Another pioneer in charting the details of the mother-infant bond has been Margaret Mahler, who, along with her associates, has provided a wealth of research in the details of how an initial symbiosis between mother and infant is formed; the various phases and subphases of this symbiotic attachment, and the relative significance of maximum accessibility of the mother in each of these subphases; the normal processes of separation-individuation out of this symbiosis; and the various psychopathologies that grow out of disturbances in all of these stages. The most succinct account of this research is provided in Mahler and Pine (1975), *The Psychological Birth of the Human Infant*.

Mahler has demonstrated that in two different kinds of infantile psychosis, there has been a failure in the early bonding of infant and mother. In autism, the symbiotic bond never developed, and in symbiotic psychosis, there has been a failure at the symbiotic stage, a premature rupture of the bond, or a failure at the separation-individuation stage, resulting in a delusional symbiotic omnipotent fusion with the mother (1972, p. 403f. offers a brief presentation).

> In either event, these children are deficient in the capacity to use the mother as a beacon of orientation in the world of reality....The result is that the infant personality fails to organize itself around the relationship to the

> mother as an external love object. The ego apparatuses, which usually grow in the matrix of the "ordinary devoted" mothering relationship...fail to thrive, or in Glover's terms..., the ego nuclei do not integrate, but secondarily fall apart (Mahler and Pine, 1975, p. 7).

Mahler's research confirmed her hypothesis of "the universality of the symbiotic origin of the human condition, as well as the hypothesis of an obligatory separation-individuation process in normal development" (1975, p. ix). In the present connection, her conclusion as to the significance of the mother's accessibility, especially during certain subphases of the separation-individuation process, is germane to my investigation:

> It is, however, the mother's continued emotional availability, we have found, that is essential if the child's autonomous ego is to attain optimal functional capacity, while his reliance on magic omnipotence recedes. If the mother is "quietly available," with a ready supply of object libido, if she shares the toddling adventurer's exploits, playfully reciprocates, and thus facilitates his salutary attempts at imitation and *identification* [italics hers], then internalization of the relation between mother and toddler is able to progress to the point where, in time, verbal communication takes over....Predictable emotional involvement on the part of the mother seems to facilitate the rich unfolding of the toddler's thought processes, reality testing, and coping behavior by the end of the second or the beginning of the third year (1975, p. 77).

Selma Fraiberg's book, *Every Child's Birthright: In Defense of Mothering*, mentioned above in connection with Klein's view of emotional development, serves as a capstone to the work of these pioneers—Bowlby, Spitz, and Mahler—in restating on behalf of all parents and children, and, indeed, on behalf of society as we know it—this unchanging and urgent matter of mother-infant bonding. Drawing on prior literature, and especially on Konrad Lorenz's study of the origins of attachment in a wide range of species and the relationship of attachment to aggressive behaviors, Fraiberg points to the peril of our failure to nourish the quality and durability of the love bonds of infancy.

In addition to pointing out the implications of the "diseases of non-attachment," mentioned above, she is able to state in very moving and self-authenticating words the reality of the "love-affair" in the mother-infant bond that underlies all later love:

The Relational Context: The Holding Environment 97

> In every act of love in mature life there is a prologue which originated in the first year of life. There are two people who arouse in each other sensual joy, feelings of longing, and the conviction that they are absolutely indispensable to each other—that life without the other is meaningless. Separation from the other is intolerable. In the wooing phase and in the prelude to the act of love, the mouth is rediscovered as an organ of pleasure and the entire skin is suffused with sensual joy. Longing seeks its oldest posture, the embrace....The discovery of the partner, the one person in the world who is the source of joy and bliss, has its origin in the discovery of the first human partner in infancy....Freud said all this seventy years ago, and there were few who believed him (1977, p. 32).

The origins of the human bonds that are the foundations of our living in the human community are to be found in this first love affair, where "the language of the eyes, the language of the smile, vocal communications of pleasure and distress" make up the rudimentary vocabulary. "The baby's rudimentary love language belongs to an inner repertoire. It is all there, potentially, in the program, but it must be elicited by a partner" (1977, p. 29).

To conclude this excursus on the matter of mother-infant bonding as it is treated in the current literature, I will mention briefly some of the factors that facilitate the building of the infant-mother bond. All of these factors have been elaborated by the authors mentioned above, and by many others.

The significance of face-to-face posture and eye contact in establishing the bond has been stressed by Robson, 1967; Riess, 1978; Stern, 1971; Bennett, 1971, to name only a few. The importance of physical contact and tactile stimulation has been thoroughly reviewed by Hong, who in surveying a broad spectrum of theoretical positions—from the psychoanalytic writers to the learning theorists—concluded that from all perspectives, "physical contact and tactile stimulation appear to be primary needs of the infant and play a crucial role in the infant's development" (Hong, 1978, p. 59). The mutual interchange between the baby's signal of distress and the mother's prompt and sensitive response of comfort as affecting the quality of the mother-child bond has also been emphasized in research findings, which have been reviewed by Judy Dunn (1977). Dunn points out that there is a growing awareness that "attachment grows through reciprocal interaction rather than through the relief of needs like hunger, that what happens in the comfortable play and exchange between mother and baby may be of crucial importance" (p. 109).

This emphasis made by Dunn on *reciprocal interaction* between mother and child is accented also by Lois Barclay Murphy (1972), who has given us a particularly rich account of the first give and take with the mother, the effects of that give and take in personality development, and the effects on a child of the deprivation of such interchange with the mother. The common emphasis of these two authors is pertinent to what a holding environment means, and therefore I want to review briefly Murphy's contribution regarding the first play of mother and baby.

Murphy understands the child's very first play to be with the nipple, where, she speculates, cognitive awareness and the earliest perceptions of the self may well be born. When the mother plays with the baby's fingers and toes, for example, Murphy says it is as though it is being communicated to the child, "There is such a lot of me and all so luscious." In this very first play, children learn to experience their own impact on the environment:

> In this earliest period, sequence of being done to and doing are close together in the mini-acts with perhaps more than mini-pleasure. As he enjoys the contact with his mother, he gradually cathects the wider environment (1972, p. 122f.).

Beginning with the gentle, tactile stimuli of the mother's care, the baby advances to rocking, bouncing, peek-a-boo, and to more complex kinesthetic-tactile-visual-auditory experiences. By four or five months, the baby may remember the bounce and invite mother to "play."

> It is precisely this actual exchange of play-signals—in cooperation with complex patterns and sequences—which the extremely deprived baby with a destitute, exhausted mother does not have, any more than do babies in some foundling homes (p. 123).

Murphy goes on to demonstrate that in such a dearth of give and take, there is no experience that leads the baby to expect pleasant results from reaching out, there is a lack of cognitive-motor-affective patterns for internalization to be later externalized in play, and, in addition, there is an absence of clear structure in time sequences and in spatial arrangements, so that the child gets stuck in exploiting sensory experience and immediate gratification over and over again.

> He cannot externalize structure he has not internalized; he cannot create new patterns with his play-things, much less develop the capacity to sublimate. Thus he is deprived of turning passive experiences into active mastery and therefore fails to develop a sense of competence beyond elementary motor skill (p. 124).

In the more fortunately mothered child, the baby begins soon to impose structure on the environment, and by about twelve months is able to turn the passive "done to" into an active "I do to you," the change that Freud saw to help the child master the stressful experience (1920, p. 16f.). Murphy describes the stages of development through the earliest months to the stage of playing a game that utilizes symbolization and structure to cope with loss, utilizing prior cognitive mastery:

> He has mastered his world enough to recreate it—and then to use the constructive potential developed in infancy for problem-solving, sublimation, and for creativity....
>
> In short it seems that not just elementary care, but active mutual mother-baby play is a pre-requisite for the development of the cognitive structuring which can carry play beyond primitive sensory-motor stages to a goal-oriented symbolic and constructive stage (p. 126).

The comments in the passage above shed light, in my view, on the deficits in the infancy of the thousands of children like William, who had no opportunity for this kind of play with mother. No wonder that our schools are full of children with learning difficulties that educators keep attacking in vain at the cognitive level. As Spitz makes plain, the affective interchange in the first human partnership is the "fundamental education," on which the ability for concept formation, word symbols, problem solving, and constructive, goal oriented tasks is founded; in Spitz's words, "All later development is predicated on it" (Spitz, 1972, p. 45).

All of the above discussion on bonding between mother and child, about this "fundamental education," brings us back to Winnicott's idea of the holding environment as the matrix for personality development, and what that holding environment involves. There is one concept of Winnicott's that offers a particularly helpful framework for our exploration of the relational context in which the young ego can flourish, a concept that he develops both around the mother-infant focus and the therapeutic focus and that may lead us to new insight about Amy, John, and William:

Ego-needs

Winnicott makes the repeated observation that the "holding" mother is not only involved in meeting the instinctual needs of the infant, that is, the need for food, warmth, tactile stimulation, alleviation of physical discomfort, and all of the other attentions required by the infant's dependency, but also is oriented to the child in such a way that she meets *the ego-needs of the child*. This idea that a baby has ego-needs as well as instinctual needs is both important and elusive, and it may be fruitful to explore its implications. What does it mean to "meet a child's ego-needs"?

The essence of this concept for me is that it means an emotional stance, an attitude, no doubt as much unconscious as conscious and which can only partially be taught, that regards the person of the infant as authentic in its own being, as respect-worthy in its own right, and as fully sufficient in its reality to emerge and flower if given the opportunity to come forth. The reality, existence, and the potential for coming into fullness is regarded as actually there in this new being, and the latent possibilities in this other are not to be made, or shaped, or forced according to the parent's own design.

On reflection, I see I am not far here from the idea of a "ground plan," perhaps even Jung's Self; there is a "given" out there, in the child, that calls for a trust on the part of the parent that this being will develop and grow according to its own inner design rather than by a pounding into a conformity with a pattern desired by the parent.

I do not wish to be misunderstood here. The issue is not one of permissiveness versus discipline. The issue is an attitude, not too far from humility, which does not assume that parenthood means the right to violate another's space, time, and being in such a way that the other is forced to comply with the parent's will. This attitude will be taken up in some detail in Chapter VIII. For the present it is sufficient to contrast this attitude of respect for a child's ego needs with the position of ignorance—which Sullivan extends to a position of "insanity"—that some parents hold in connection with childrearing. In discussing, in a most edifying way, the various misconceptions to which parents may be subject, he points to the "curious, if not subpsychotic, attempts to guide, direct, break, manage, and so on, the self-willed infant." He adds, for our instruction, an apt comment about "the disastrous effects of treating a year-old baby as if he were being deliberately troublesome" (Sullivan, 1953, p. 173). These misconceptions serve well as the negative of what it means to meet a child's ego-needs.

Winnicott's thoughts about this matter included his view that even in the earliest feeding situations it is possible to meet a child's instinctual needs while violating the ego-needs. That is to say, a mother may present the breast, or the bottle, in such a way as to impinge on the child in an intense effort to see that the baby is properly nourished, rather than to feel empathically the infant's need to find in the mother's offering his own wish-fulfillment. In a way, it is simply a matter of whose idea this feeding is.

Winnicott has worked out this idea rather elaborately, suggesting that the best arrangement is that the mother manage by sensitivity and timing to overlap with the "real" breast the child's omnipotent illusion that his wish created the breast. Winnicott, as discussed in Chapter III, understood that it is in this experience and space of "illusion" that the infant's ability to use a symbol, subsequent play and creativity, and the experience of feeling alive and real is born (1971, p. 10f.).

It is a question of whether the child's own confidence and creative impulse is being nourished in this early give and take with the other, or whether there is felt on the part of the child a necessity to move back in the face of intrusive encroachment by the mother's handling. There is a reminder here of Erikson's view of the mutuality in relationship *"which strengthens the doer even as it strengthens the other,..in whatever strength is appropriate to his age, stage, and condition"* (1964, p. 233). [Italics his.] Erikson states:

> I would call mutuality a relationship in which partners depend on each other for the development of their respective strengths. A baby's first responses can be seen as part of an actuality consisting of many details of mutual arousal and response. While the baby initially smiles at a mere configuration resembling a human face, the adult cannot help smiling

back, filled with expectations of a "recognition" which he needs to secure from the new being as surely as it needs him. The fact is that the mutuality of adult and baby is the original source of hope, the basic ingredient of all effective as well as ethical human action. As far back as 1895, Freud confronts the "helpless" new-born infant with a "help-rich ("hilfreich") adult, and postulates that their mutual understanding is "the primal source of all moral motives" (1964, p. 231).

Among the many rich insights Winnicott has contributed around this general theme of meeting ego-needs, there are two that have been particularly enlightening to me and that may be pertinent in pursuing the questions raised at the end of Chapter I. The first of these ideas is the mirroring role of the parent, and the second is the matter of handling ambivalence in parent-child relationships. Let us explore these two ideas.

Mirror-role of mother and family

Winnicott emphasized the role of the mother—extending to the father, the rest of the family, and the larger environment—as mirror to the children, that is, the one who reflects back to them their own authentic existence (1971, p. 111f.). This reflection back to the child begins with the baby's looking into the mother's face. (See also Erikson, 1964, p. 102; Riess, 1978, p. 383f.). In effect, the infant sees a self-reflection there. If the mother is looking at her baby, her own face bears an image. The image may impart different messages; it may communicate, for example, "You are infinitely beautiful and important," or "You are ugly and troublesome," "You make me tense and irritable, and I wish you would hurry," or any of a number of other feelings that the mother conveys.

In other words, the baby gets the first external confirmation of the ego or the first rejection from this experience of watching mother's face in the feeding situation. If she is habitually tense, anxious, irritable, the self is first seen in this light; if she is unresponsive, "then a mirror is a thing to be looked at but not looked into" (Winnicott, 1971, p. 113). If it "notices and approves," then surely the person reflected there is a real and worthy being. When one is seen, one knows one exists. Winnicott posits the historical process this way:

> When I look I am seen, so I exist.
> I can now afford to look and see.
> I now look creatively and what I apperceive I also perceive.
> In fact I take care not to see what is not there to be seen....(1971, p. 114).

Winnicott observes that the mirror role of the mother, as it expands into an ever widening circle from the family to the community at large, plays an important part in ego development throughout life. He sees it also as central in psychotherapy:

> Psychotherapy is not making clever and apt interpretations; by and large it is a long-term giving the patient back what the patient brings. It is a complex derivative of the face that reflects what is there to be seen. I like to think of my work this way, and to think that if I do this well enough the patient will find his or her own self, and will be able to exist and to feel real (1971, p. 117).

In my own therapeutic work, I have found this insight invariably fruitful. My first task with children in play therapy, and, for a while, almost my only task, is to recognize and mirror back a child's own being. Any child, but especially one who has been deprived of such recognition, will rejoice in this experience of being seen. Hiding under a table or blanket, for example, makes a delightful opportunity to show one small part of one's self at a time, just to have it seen and responded to. I may find myself saying something like this:

> Where is Johnny? Hm, I don't see him—he's gone. Oh wait, I see a foot—right there. Oh, now it's gone. Oh say, there is a hand—there is an elbow. Aha, there now is a leg—a right leg, now a left. Oh say, there is Johnny's head. There is a face—Johnny's face, and it's laughing at me!

Thinking back to Amy, John, and William, I believe that reflecting back to each child the spontaneous gesture was central in the work. With all three, it was the unspoken message, there from the beginning, that I was there as the follower, and not the leader, of their reaching out toward new horizons that communicated the attitude of respect for *their own being*, and this stance called forth something previously dormant in the children, enabling them to chart new seas for themselves. The attitude of waiting, seeing, appreciating—but not praising—what the children do is the very essence of the therapeutic work. This unspoken attitude meets the children's ego needs, their feeling that they have in themselves the capacity to create, to enlarge their boundaries, to claim undeveloped potency.

This point may be made clearer by speculating, for example, what would have happened, when Amy sketched out the first tentative lines of her house plan, if I had abandoned my position of mirror and had instead endeavored to offer helpful suggestions as to how she might improve the house. Had I impinged on her own spontaneous gesture, either by questions or by interpretations, she would no doubt have moved back to a position of greater safety for her ego's needs instead of coming out more boldly with each new bit of her creation. It was her own efforts toward discovering her whole being, her real house, that needed to be sustained by my attentive acceptance and respect. This attitude of sustaining and supporting the other's own being will be explored further in Chapter VIII.

The formulation of Winnicott's—the mirror role of the parent—gave me a way to conceptualize one route by which the ego of the child becomes strengthened. If children do something, or, even if they only experience something passively, finding that the experience is mirrored back to them by the attentive parent seems to strengthen the happening and to make it more real.

Something as simple as saying to a child who is struggling with a car track that keeps coming apart, "That track is giving you trouble today," suggests that there is someone seeing things as the child sees them, and the perception of the thing itself, and of the self as perceiver and actor is magnified. It is as though the child can have the ego experience twice—once in the doing or in the perceiving, and a second time in having someone see and reflect it. In addition, children may begin to see bits and pieces of themselves, through this kind of reflection, of which they had been unaware, and thus to integrate into the ego fragments of experience that contribute to a sense of self (Winnicott, 1971, p. 64).

Thus, one important aspect of the holding environment, in terms of meeting ego-needs, is this responsibility of the adult to be present to the child in such a way that the child's own reality, own creativity, and own authentic being is faithfully recognized and reflected.

Ambivalence of mother and family.

The second way in which I feel particularly indebted to Winnicott in my own thinking about the holding environment as meeting ego-needs has to do with the necessity for parents to come to terms with the facts of life concerning ambivalence. That is to say, that all loving, including maternal loving, includes negative feelings, aggression, and—in the opinion of many respect-worthy psychoanalytic writers, including both Winnicott and Harold Searles—"hate" as well. Does the holding environment for a nascent ego include hate? I admit that I am not at all sure about the word "hate," but that ambivalence, anger, and aggression must be dealt with in every significant relationship, including the mother-infant one, I have no doubt, and I would like to investigate the implications of this statement for personality development and sublimation.

Winnicott assaults rather effectively our tendency to deny that hate is a part of loving parental relationship in his paper, "Hate in the Countertransference" (1947, p. 194f.). He lists some twenty or so reasons as to why a mother has cause to hate her baby, reasons that are entertaining as well as thought-provoking. For example,

> His excited love is cupboard love, so that having got what he wants he throws her away like an orange peel.
> He is ruthless, treats her as scum, an unpaid servant, a slave.
> He is suspicious, refuses her good food, and makes her doubt herself, but eats well with his aunt.

As capstone of his argument that hate is an ingredient of parental love, he reminds us of the timeless lullaby that mothers sing:

> Rockabye Baby, on the tree top,
> When the wind blows the cradle will rock,
> When the bough breaks the cradle will fall,
> Down will come baby, cradle and all.
> He states:

> I think of a mother (or father) playing with a small infant; the infant enjoying the play and not knowing that the parent is expressing hate in the words, perhaps in terms of birth symbolism. This is not a sentimental rhyme. Sentimentality is useless for parents, as it contains a denial of hate,

and sentimentality in a mother is no good at all from the infant's point of view.

It seems to me doubtful whether a human child as he develops is capable of tolerating the full extent of his own hate in a sentimental environment. He needs hate to hate (1947, p. 202).

Winnicott's view of hate and aggression, repeatedly expressed, is that it is these feelings that make it possible for the individual to perceive the quality of *externality*, that is, it is aggression that makes the outside real and separate from the inside world. He considers it this way:

It is legitimate...to say that at whatever age a baby begins to allow the breast an external position (outside the area of projection), then this means that destruction of the breast has become a feature. I mean the actual impulse to destroy. It is an important part of what a mother does, to be the first person to take the baby through this first version of the many that will be encountered, of attack that is survived (1971, p. 92).[1]

He summarizes:

The assumption is always there, in orthodox theory, that aggression is reactive to the encounter with the reality principle, whereas here it is the destructive drive that creates the quality of externality....

The object is always being destroyed....The destructiveness, plus the object's survival of the destruction, places the object outside the area of objects set up by the subject's projective mental mechanisms. In this way a world of shared reality is created which the subject can use and which can feed back other-than-me substance into the subject (1971, p. 93f.).

Harold Searles, an analyst who has contributed greatly to our understanding of schizophrenia, as well as to the broader range of psychiatric disorders, also stresses the interrelatedness of love and hate. Searles stated that families can be crippled and paralyzed by their inability to come to terms with their ambivalence:

---

[1] Winnicott's thought here sheds light on what was happening in the therapeutic work of the child described as moving from ruthlessness to concern: his destructiveness toward me was a way of establishing my external reality through my survival of his attack.

> Only in so far as the therapist can help them to face both their love and their hatred can they relinquish the symbiotic mode of relatedness which is serving their family-wide unconscious defence against this ambivalence, but which is thwarting, by the very nature of this relatedness, their development of ego maturity and genuine object relatedness with one another (Searles, 1965, p. 738).

As does Winnicott, Searles associates hate and destructiveness with the ability to feel that one is a separate person and points out that both in severe psychopathology and in normal development ambivalence is a central dynamic force. In discussing the schizophrenic child, he says:

> ...The core of his personality remains unformed, and ego-fragmentation and dedifferentiation become powerful, through deeply primitive, unconscious defences against the awareness of ambivalence in the object and in himself. Even in normal development, one becomes a separate person only by becoming able to face, and accept ownership of, one's ambivalent feelings of love and hate towards the other person (1965, p. 524).

About the usefulness of the ingredient of hate in psychotherapy, he says:

> I find a generous place in psychotherapy for all the sadism I can muster—for example, to needle and infuriate the apathetic or 'out-of-contact' patient into more overt relatedness, or to pay him back for the hurts he has been inflicting upon me. With an abundance of this kind of interaction between us, he has good reason to know that I am in no wise a saint, and we can deal with his own problems about sadism in a person-to-person fashion (Searles, 1965, p. 25).

However, Searles emphasizes that although love and hate are inevitably interrelated, in the final analysis the hateful feelings must be subordinated to the loving feelings in order for the ego to grow (1965, p. 220).[2]

In the attempt to understand the nature of the containing relationships that foster sublimation and personality growth, it is my view that

---

[2] A similar view has been expressed by Michael Balint in "Love and Hate" (1952).

the problems of ambivalence are central. The passages above raise a number of questions about parents and children—and therapists and patients—in regard to the why, as well as to the whence and whither of ambivalence. Therefore, in the next chapter, I want to address some of the implications of the presence of negative as well as positive feelings in the human condition in general, and in Amy, John, and William in particular.

Chapter VI

AMBIVALENCE: SOME IMPLICATIONS FOR AMY, JOHN, AND WILLIAM

Winnicott and Searles, in their emphasis on negative as well as positive feelings as central in family relationships, are referring, in my view, to a basic dialectic in human experience involving *opposites*, which, in different ways, was germane to the thought of both Freud and Jung. While Jung thought of the dialectic in terms of tension between opposites as being the source of psychic energy and as fundamental to all understanding of the psyche—both collective and personal—, Freud perceived the dialectic in terms of conflict: conflict, for example, between the pleasure principle and the reality principle, between love and hate, between conscious and unconscious, but primarily between "elemental instincts...manifested almost from the first in pairs of opposites...which is termed ambivalence of feeling" (1915, p. 281 of S.E., 14, offers alternate translation).

Pushed to its final formulation, Freud conceptualized the "death instincts" versus the "libidinal instincts" as the ultimate polarity of opposites, and he spoke of the entire evolution of culture as the working out in the human and social drama of the "struggle between

Eros and Death, between the instincts of life and the instincts of destruction as it works itself out in the human species" (1929, p. 122).

While Freud's introduction of the death instinct into his theory (1920) was fundamentally an attempt to bring his observations about instincts into a biological framework through pursuing an explanation of certain phenomena that did not seem to fit into his libido theory— i.e., evidences of what he termed the "repetition compulsion"—, the long-term impact of this major revision of his theory has been mainly in terms of a corollary to the death instinct, namely aggression as a separate drive. From the point of this major revision in Freud's theory, aggression as an entity fully as significant in human nature as sexuality has been generally accepted in psychoanalytic thought. Freud's own way of stating the matter was:

> The inclination to aggression is an original, self-subsisting instinctual disposition in man....This aggressive instinct is the derivative and the main representative of the death instinct which we have found alongside of Eros and which shares world-dominion with it (1929, p. 122).

The presence of aggression in human beings does not need to be documented, nor does the question of its original source, for the purpose of this inquiry, need to be settled here. The necessity for it, even for us to be able to love, has been fairly well established, and the usefulness of it in the business of living in general has been frequently affirmed.[1] Consider the following thoughts about some of the reasons we need aggression:

> Aggression is needed to differentiate the ego from its unconscious matrix, to find an ego stance and an ego value and to develop them to maturity. Aggression is needed to establish one's place in relation to others, to accept one's limits and not be daunted by them. Aggression is also needed to assert the ego's wishes against others' opinions, so that one is not overwhelmed every time another person or one's own superego disapproves. The ego needs aggression to find a flexible self-reliance that can face up to others' disapproval and cooperate with them even if one does not agree with them. Only when a person can consciously channel his aggression in these various ways will he be open to values beyond himself.

---

[1] Adrian Stokes, whose work has been referred to, spoke of the function of the death instinct in the human capacity for refusal, resignation, and acceptance in the integrative processes of human life and the respect for reason and reality (Stokes, 1973c, p. 68f.).

For only then will there be an ego available to open and the energy to make the effort and sustain it (Ulanov, 1975, p. 180).

Phyllis Greenacre, whose rich insights into human development, gathered over decades of psychoanalytic practice, have now been collected into two volumes (1971), has written of the significance of aggression in the unfolding of the human person from the very beginning, of its connection with creativity and the feeling of being alive, its function in the person's defensive processes, and its connection with virtually all aspects of life, including, e.g., playing, weeping, and giving birth. She provides us with a memorable image in connection with her view of aggression as a developmental force, which she quotes from a friend:

> When I see the crocuses and the snowdrops pushing their way through the frozen earth at the end of winter, I am appalled at the fierceness of the tender shoots. It would take a swing of a pick-axe to do as good a job (Greenacre, 1957, p. 63).

The fact of aggression and the usefulness of it seem to be conspicuous enough; some of the problems connected with it, however, are more difficult; for example, its connection with various degrees of destructiveness and hostility, which can be turned against one's self as against one's neighbor, and its capacity for various transformations, including the guise of conscience and morality (Freud, e.g., 1917c, 1923, 1924a, 1929). The task now at hand is to address some of these problems with aggression, especially in regard to what happens to ambivalence in parent-child relationships.

Problems Connected With Aggression

A great deal of Freud's work, especially after 1920, was concerned with the thorny questions raised by aggression. One way he addressed these questions was by theorizing that the two instincts—the libidinal instinct, Eros, and the destructive instinct, Thanatos—were in normality fused with each other:

> Now it seems as though an instinct of the one sort can scarcely ever operate in isolation; it is always accompanied—or, as we say, alloyed—with a certain quota from the other side, which modifies its aim or is, in some

cases, what enables it to achieve that aim. Thus, for instance, the instinct of self-preservation is certainly of an erotic kind, but it must nevertheless have aggressiveness at its disposal if it is to fulfill its purpose. So, too, the instinct of love, when it is directed towards an object, stands in need of some contribution from the instinct for mastery if it is in any way to obtain possession of that object. The difficulty of isolating the two classes of instinct in their actual manifestations is indeed what has so long prevented us from recognizing them (1932, p. 209f.).

And elsewhere:

We perceive that for purposes of discharge the instinct of destruction is habitually brought into the service of Eros...and we come to understand that instinctual defusion and the marked emergence of the death instinct call for particular consideration among the effects of some severe neuroses—for instance, the obsessional neurosis (1923, p. 41f.).

The conclusive evidence for some kind of fusion between the two instinctual forces Freud found in the puzzling phenomenon of masochism. He identified here the coalescence of an erotic lust for pain and the punitive sadism in the superego's attack on the ego. Among the different forms of masochism, he pointed to moral masochism as the finishing stroke for his argument:

Thus moral masochism becomes a classical piece of evidence for the existence of fusion of instinct. Its danger lies in the fact that it originates from the death instinct and corresponds to the part of that instinct which has escaped being turned outwards as an instinct of destruction. But since, on the other hand, it has the significance of an erotic component, even the subject's destruction of himself cannot take place without libidinal satisfaction (Freud, 1924a, p. 170).

The question arises as to whether the children's play, as we observed it in Chapter I, confirms in any way this theory of Freud's, and later I will respond to that question. At this point, it is pertinent to add to Freud's comments about fusion of instincts a contribution of René Spitz in a discussion of the effects of object loss on children who are deprived of mothering:

The infants suffering from marasmus had been deprived of the opportunity to form object relations. Consequently they had not been able to direct the libidinal drive and the aggressive drive onto one and the same object—the indispensable prerequisite toward achieving the fusion of the two drives. Deprived of an object in the external world, the unfused drives were turned against their own person, which they took as object....

In my opinion, in the normal state of fusion of the two drives, aggression plays a role which is comparable to that of a carrier wave. In this way the impetus of aggression makes it possible to direct both drives toward the surround. But if the aggressive and the libidinal drives do not achieve fusion, or alternatively, if a defusion has taken place, then aggression is returned against his own person; and in this case libido also can no longer be directed toward the outside (Spitz, 1965, p. 288).

Spitz, in line with Freud, is addressing the issue of fusion of instincts in connection with this strange problem of destructiveness turned against the self.

Destructiveness against the self is a matter Amy and John are going further to illuminate. First, however, it is important to explore briefly one aspect of this destructiveness that may enlarge our understanding of their contribution: that is, Freud's discovery of the paradox that aggression against the self is heightened by the very attempt to renounce aggression.

The more a man controls his aggressiveness, the more intense becomes his inclination to aggressiveness against his own ego (1923, p. 54).

The attempt to renounce aggression, to banish it from our dealings with others, is attractive to many of us, and it is sobering to be confronted with the idea that it is an unsuccessful solution to the matter, that disclaiming aggression does not eliminate it.

There is a sting in this statement of Freud's aimed at advocates of moral idealism who assume that destructive aggression can be subordinated at will to high standards of conduct. Freud confronts us with a most thought-provoking comment in discussing this issue—the limitations of moral aspiration in dealing with instinctual drives.

The formation of an ego ideal is often confused with the sublimation of instinct, to the detriment of our understanding of the facts. A man who has exchanged his narcissism for homage to a high ego ideal has not necessarily on that account succeeded in sublimating his libidinal instincts. It is true that the ego ideal demands such sublimation, but it cannot enforce it; sublimation remains a special process which may be prompted by the ideal but the execution of which is entirely independent of any such prompting....As we have learnt, the formation of an ideal heightens the demand of the ego and is the most powerful factor favoring repression; sublimation is a way out, a way by which those demands can be met *without* involving repression (1914, p. 94f.). [Italics his.]

This passage represents an early conception of what Freud would later call the superego. In this paper, "On Narcissism," he posits a kind of "gradation in the ego" from the standpoint of which one measures himself, an ego ideal "which is now the target of the self-love which was enjoyed in childhood by the actual ego" (p. 94). Parenthetically, in developing this new idea, Freud further undermines the moralistic position by suggesting that pursuit of idealistic standards of behavior—homage to a high ego ideal—is primarily a narcissistic, as distinguished from an altruistic, undertaking:

> As always where the libido is concerned, man has here again shown himself incapable of giving up a satisfaction he had once enjoyed. He is not willing to forgo the narcissistic perfection of his childhood; and when, as he grows up, he is disturbed by the admonitions of others and by the awakening of his own critical judgement, so that he can no longer retain that perfection, he seeks to recover it in the new form of an ego ideal. What he projects before him as his ideal is the substitute for the lost narcissism of his childhood in which he was his own ideal (Freud, 1914, p. 94).

The point clearly emerges that attempted renunciation of negative feelings in the interest of idealism is, in addition to the humbling revelation that it is an ego-centric endeavor to gain favor in one's own eyes, "the most powerful factor favoring repression." As Freud learned, and as is now self-evident, repression does not bring us far forward in the transformation of instinctual impulses. In Jung's phrase, the unconscious can simply "gain an unassailable ascendancy," and "wield an attractive force that can invalidate all conscious contents" (Jung, CW, 7, p. 344). Aggressive forces under repression will "out"; if not directly, then in neurotic or psychotic symptoms. They will return in our very efforts to defend against them and belie their most hostile nature. Who has not been on both the giving and receiving end of lethal kindness?

Freud's later work on the superego demonstrates again and again that the very destructiveness and sadism that is repressed under its aegis reinvades the repressing agency and may return under more deadly form under the mask of righteousness than in its original form.

Many of us do not have to look far within to discover that we live with a version of the Grand Inquisitor, and the torments it can mete out make quite understandable Freud's shrewd observation that the superego is potentially cruel; it originates from the id and partakes of its essential nature (1926, p. 115f.).

Erik Erikson contributes further to this line of thought by addressing the fact that "the radical division into good and bad can be *the* sickness of the mind":

> The voice of the super-ego is not always cruel and derisive, but it is ever ready to become so whenever the precarious balance which we call a good conscience is upset, at which times the secret weapons of this inner governor are revealed: the brand of shame and the bite of conscience....
>
> All we know for certain is that the moral proclivity in man does not develop without the establishment of some chronic self-doubt and some truly terrible—even if largely submerged—rage against anybody and anything that reinforces such doubt. The "lowest" in man is thus apt to reappear in the guise of the "highest." Irrational and pre-rational combinations of goodness, doubt, and rage can re-emerge in the adult in those malignant forms of righteousness and prejudice which we may call *moralism*. In the name of high moral principles all the vindictiveness of derision, or torture, and of mass extinction can be employed. One surely must come to the conclusion that the Golden Rule was meant to protect man not only against his enemy's open attacks, but also against his friend's righteousness (1964, p. 223f.). [Italics his.]

Aggression routed through the superego, in the way presented so forcefully by Freud and Erikson was, in my view, the element that caused the most difficulty for both Amy and John. Let us look first, however, at William, where the problem of aggression is more transparent.

Aggression: William

"I'm good at hitting people in the face; that's what I'm good at." William's aggression was in plain view because it was directed against the outside world and was *undercontrolled* because of an early failure in the meeting of his ego-needs by what Spitz would call a deficiency in the parental presence; mother was not there, and therefore there was insufficient opportunity to appropriate an internal object, in Klein's vocabulary. Consequently, William lacked the ability to control his own instinctual urges. There was no effective superego at all, and it was understandable that this little boy felt such kinship with that poor horse who kept knocking everything down in his path, and with the bad little monkey who kept getting himself in trouble and was so much in need of a rescuer. He had no "man in the yellow hat," no firm and friendly object on the inside, no "good internal object," to use Klein's phrase, or no "beacon in the world," to use Mahler's phrase, to help him control his aggression.[2]

That William found his way to put a "man with the yellow hat" on the inside through the route of the dough, which without doubt represented for him the good breast, is a confirmation both of Klein's view that the opportunity to internalize the good breast through the tender ministrations of the mother is the first indispensable step in adequate personality structure, and Winnicott's view of the transitional object as the means of making the good object portable for himself.

William also makes a connection for us with Sechehaye's concept of "symbolic realization," discussed in Chapter III, to which Winnicott refers also (e.g., 1962, p. 60). William had a fundamental need, a hunger, that was fulfilled, or met, through provision of a potentially appropriatable symbol made possible through a mothering one and affectively connected with her.

As we have seen, Winnicott's view of the matter was somewhat different from Sechehaye's, in that for him it was the child's wish, the fulfillment of which was "realized," rather than the case that it was the symbol that was realized. Either way, the substance of the matter is that it is via the symbol, provided initially by the provision of the good breast—in its largest sense—that the child's deep need is fulfilled or realized.

William traversed in his route a way to finding a "man in the yellow hat" inside, who could help him manage his destructive aggression; to

---

[2] Spitz (1958) contributes three "primordia" of the superego that derive from the parental presence: 1) the physical intervention of the parent, 2) the parent's positive example, which in affective interchange becomes meaningful for the child, and 3) the "identification with the aggressor" at the level of the formation of the ego ideal. "All three have in common the wish to identify with the love object at all cost" (p. 393f.).

use his other literary image, he found a way to bring that tyrannical sneeze of Robert, the horse, into police service. He found that good friend inside by means of the dough, which connected him to the friend who was in the room with him. It was by means of the dough and the cake that William found the inner authority to line up all those wild animals, run down each with his car, and say, "There is going to be a new street, and they are in the way."

Thus does a child state in poetry what more prosaic clinicians would state as the neutralization of impulse through the expansion of ego functions through the incorporation of certain aspects of the therapist. That impulse material has been put at the service of the ego instead of the service of the id is indeed more powerfully stated by William simply as "a new street."

Aggression: Amy and John

With Amy and John, the problem of aggression was just as severe as with William, but the aggression came through the route of the superego. It was the sadism of the moral agency that was most troublesome to them. Let us reconsider, for example, Amy's dreams:

> My face was invisible. I had to wear a mask. Then they finally found out I had a mask. Then my face came back.
>
> I was being chased by a monster;..there were roots of a big tree all over the ground, and I kept tripping and falling. I had to keep getting up and running around.
>
> There was a big dog; it kept jumping and jumping on me.

We now know something new about the monster that was after Amy. That monster compelled her to wear a mask; to hide her feelings; to substitute nervous tics for the expression of bad feelings; to isolate parts of herself in a doghouse, far removed from her living space; to keep getting up and running around in a ceaseless effort to please her elders; to withdraw, for relief, from the world of people into the world of books.

This monster was aggression—and it was *her* aggression, all right—, but it was primarily aggression turned against her ego by the superego.

That big dog that kept jumping and jumping on her represented, at least in part, this same variety of aggression; it was attacking her most viciously through the severity, the overcontrol, of the internalized moral agency.

Perhaps that overcontrol underlay the reference in her very first play scene to anger at an oppressive overlord: "The Americans are very angry with the British because of all the bad things the British did." Maybe it was that same anger that caused her to need a larger toilet in her house, a larger facility for elimination of some of the anger that later found expression in word pictures of "Bang," and "Rip," and fireworks on display. The little girl with flaming red cheeks and that bad, devouring snake that "could kill us, you know" told us something about her anger at an oppressive overlord more severe that her real mother ever was—her own superego.

Amy undertook a long search for containers. Why did she so urgently need containers? Surely she was looking for places to put some of the feelings that were beginning to get loosed from repression, i.e., loosed from the tight restraining hold of the superego. Her compelling imagery that progressed from a closed box—to cages with doors—to an open bird bath gave us hints along the way that a relenting overlord was beginning to untie the fetters and give her room to breathe.

The changing configuration of dark and light spots on that dog, which at first was "fat and kind of ugly," had something to do with an alleviation of the destructive criticality of the superego against the child's image of herself, her "self-regard," to use Freud's phrase. I might speculate that the theme of the bigger house, which occupied Amy so constantly through her journey, had reference to the growth of her own ego as it was progressively freed from the stunting effects of the aggressivity of her own moral agency. Little by little, Amy was discovering new pieces of herself that contributed to nobler dwellings. There will be occasion to say more about her expressions of this growth later on.

What about the problem of aggression in John? At first glance, one would not see this quiet, restrained young fellow as having difficulty with aggression; "hitting people in the face" was certainly not his problem. However, taking a closer look, we can find aggression at the heart of his trouble—the aggression, once more, of the moral agency.

Ambivalence: Some Implications for Amy, John, and William

Let's begin with his statement, "He's always going forward, but his car is always left behind." Why would a boy in his going forth into the world leave his power behind? That is, indeed, what John was doing in his giving up on races and failing in the classroom; he was leaving his power behind.

He pointed toward an answer to this question himself when he referred to certain risks involved in the pursuit of power. When an Indian warrior was swallowed up in a trap during an attempt to take a fort, John sounded the moral: "This is what can happen to you if you want to be first." When a warrior met death in battle, his gravestone was inscribed, "Too fast and too good." Clearly, the motive for leaving one's power behind would be fear. Fear of what, of whom? What was the force that confronted this child, apparently, with a threat to his very life unless he left his power behind?

From one point of view, the danger had a reference to a figure in the real world; that is, at one level the drama can be read in terms of the classical oedipal triangle in its original form. In this framework, there is always the fear in the son that if he supersedes the father, the father will retaliate against him. This fear is generalized, or can be generalized, to all competitive situations: "to win," in the unconscious, could mean winning the mother, defeating the father, thus making oneself vulnerable to the retaliative vengeance of this stronger figure. Competition would therefore be fraught with danger because it is associatively connected with this primordial triangle.

Thus, danger from the external world can be the source, at one level, of fear of claiming one's own power.

However, as Freud stressed in his last work (1940), and, as his daughter, Anna, also emphasized and applied to her special work on normality and pathology in childhood (1946, 1965), the external world is only one battlefront for the ego; there are two more sources of danger.

On the one hand, there is the danger threatening from one's own instinctual urges: the threat that these forces could, after all, get out of hand and overrun the ego. Here too, there may be an unconscious generalization that complicates matters. Any self-assertion, any show of strength at all, may be sensed by the ego as being connected with destructive and malign urges and therefore represent danger.

Would danger from this quarter—along with the danger from the external world—shed light perhaps, on John's repeated dramas of robbery and murder? Did assertion to him feel, indeed, like murder, and threaten him from the direction of the id, to use Freud's language? And what about the theme of the "mud"? Was the mud perhaps his own anger, in which he was in danger of sinking—again a danger from the direction of his own impulse? John did say, "For two days, he was just a blob of mud; he couldn't even move at first. If he had stayed like that any longer, he would have hardened, and he would have been just a statue." That mud, that "quicksand," as he also described it, may have had reference to unstable terrain also in the real world; however, I suggest that his fear was sinking into and being stuck in his own anger, what he felt to be his own bad part, his own destructive urges. A second source of danger to John has been identified, a second reason "to leave his car behind."

The third source of danger, the third battlefront, is the danger from the superego, or the internalized representative of the first danger, the real father. However, as we have now seen in the work of Freud, and especially in the work of Klein, this internal object—deriving as it does from the real parent, the child's own instinctual urges superimposed on his perceptions of the parental handling, and the exaggerated quality of both of these as they are intensified by the derivatives of life and death instincts in his own ambivalence—can be ferocious far beyond the original external object, that is, the real parent. It is in this internal representation that the aggression constellates itself in such power and plays those tricks to which Freud pointed: those tricks of turning around on the self, of hiding in guises of virtue; of attacking the ego through the very defense against it in exaggerated, persecutory ways.[3]

Where, in John's story, is this third enemy of owning his car, his power, revealed? Clearly, it is revealed in his reduced self-regard, in the depletion of the libido in the ego, to use Freud's formulation (1914, p. 98). John's small hero looked "so weird." "There's something weird about him." The fellow soldiers kept asking, "What's wrong with you? Why is your coat falling off?" "We never did decide," he said, "what is

---

[3] The psychoanalytic view that bestial forces from the id may invade the sphere of conscience and ruthlessly oppress the ego from two directions has a Biblical analogy, in which "rebellious beasts," no longer in subjection to man as in the original order of creation, became in time the source of the beast-like figures of the apocalypse, where animals represent spiritual powers (Barrett, 1962, p. 10).

wrong with this soldier, whether it was a mistake,..or whether the sleeve got torn in battle."

Also, this little soldier "fainted so often I don't know why they put him in"; and "he had no sword at all." While these self-references are not unrelated to the two dangers mentioned above—that is, the necessity to stay self-reduced out of danger from the external world and out of the danger that one's own impulses might get out of hand—, I am emphasizing that this reduced self-regard required large amounts of aggression turned against the ego in the form of self-criticism. The depletion in the vital supplies to the child's ego-needs, to use the term introduced above, which seemed to derive from the superego's attacks on the ego, underlies the child's repeated concern for a little figure "who had nearly drowned for lack of oxygen."

It was the aggression from the superego that kept this child feeling small and insignificant, that kept him feeling passive and helpless, and in need of rescue. "It was cold on the desert at night and hot in the daytime" is a poignant reference to the degree of discomfort this child suffered at the hands of a severe internal critic. The "swords of the powerful enemy," planted in the sand in such a way that insurgents were in imminent danger of death by falling on them, no doubt has a reference to the fear of the real father, but it is my view that the more profound reference is to the internalized parent, the potentially brutal superego.

Such fears in the mind of a child cannot be far from Freud's death instinct and incline one to agree with those who perceive that something more is involved in such inner conflict than mere derivatives from experience with the outside world. Adrian Stokes, mentioned above, stated such a view in this way:

> I myself cannot avoid the conclusion that the ego has been educated, and indeed initiated, in more than one school (1973a, p. 56).

Stokes reminds us in the article from which this statement is taken that Melanie Klein found a considerable part of the death instinct to be lodged in the superego, and that Freud observed the same thing in regard to the melancholic (Stokes, 1973a, p. 63). I believe that the child, John, has corroborated these views in his play.

And what of the outcome of John's play? Did his imagery reveal any alleviation of the destructiveness turned against his ego? His drawing, mentioned above, of a horned spirit looming above a house, with the inscription, "This is a spirit coming to this house," gives us a clue to this question. This boy who spoke who spoke at first of a car that was always going forward and leaving its power behind has conceived an image that conveys a different message, a figure of conspicuous potency. A change has come about in John's self-regard.

Implications for the Parent-Child Relationship of These Problems Connected With Aggression

The question may now be asked: What have Amy and John to offer in the way of insight to parents into the problems of ambivalence in their relationships with their children?

At the outset it needs to be made clear that we are not dealing, in this issue, with matters that are handled even primarily at the conscious level. The most sobering aspect of familial—and, indeed, all human—relationship is that unconscious factors are at least as significant as the conscious, and perhaps more so.

Let us consider, for example, the connection between the parent's superego and the ego of the child. What happens if the parent has a seriously deficient superego, as a result of inadequate object relations in his own childhood? The child, in all probability, will suffer the same deficiency in his own inner authority. And what happens if the parent is burdened with an overly severe internal moral agency? Since that condition has been the focus of the discussion above, I want to explore further this part of the issue.

A young patient, an eleven-year-old boy who suffered from a savagely cruel inner critic, provides us with a most revealing statement in answer to the last question. His young hero was always finding himself imprisoned—now by wild bandits—now by some very strict "block people." It seemed clear enough that the wild bandits represented his own aggressive impulses, and I had a hunch that certain qualities of rigidity in those block people represented on the outside some of the aspects of his severe overlord on the inside. When I asked him if he could tell me something more about the block people, he replied with conviction, "Well, you see, they sacrifice everything to their gods, and they were going to sacrifice him too."

Ambivalence: Some Implications for Amy, John, and William 123

    This child was referring, in my view, to the fact that aggression that is harbored in a severe parental superego extends its sadism to the child and has a potentially deleterious effect on the child's ego development. This statement is meant to indicate a more direct effect than is to be explained by the fact that parents with severe superegos may tend toward external severity toward the child; actually, that direct harshness may or may not occur on the surface. I am also suggesting that there is something beyond the child's inevitable imitation of the parent, the patterning by identification of the child's ego according to the model presented him by the parent, so that the child of an extremely self-critical parent will learn, by example, how to be self-critical. A further dimension of the matter has to do with an implication of Freud's insight that the narcissism of the parent is shared with the child.

    Because the idea of narcissism is easily subject to misunderstanding, that is, it is so often taken only in a superficial sense, I want to turn briefly to Freud's thought about it in order to see what light it sheds on the question at hand.

Narcissism: Parents and Children

    Freud's characteristic willingness to allow clinical evidence to alter his theoretical formulations led him in 1914 to make a first major revision of his theory of the libido. Having observed that certain phenomena in schizophrenia, in organic illness, in sleep, in hypochondria, and in certain other situations, such as falling in love, did not fit into his previous view that the libido emanated exclusively from the id toward objects, he now posited that the libido also hovers around, or is attached to, or one could say, is invested in, the ego itself.

    While this theory in itself is quite interesting and far-reaching in its implications, the importance of it in the present connection is Freud's observation that this libido that hovers around one's own ego is shared with, or extends to, one's children. He makes a convincing case for the truth of his assertion in the following passage. Because his thought about it is so fundamental a link in my own train of thought about how the superego of the parent is connected to ego of the child, I will quote it nearly in its entirety:

> If we look at the attitude of affectionate parents toward their children, we have to recognize that it is a revival and reproduction of their own narcissism, which they have long since abandoned. The trustworthy pointer constituted by overevaluation...dominates...their emotional attitude. Thus they are under a compulsion to ascribe every perfection to the child—which sober observation would find no occasion to do—and to conceal and forget all his shortcomings....The child shall have a better time than his parents; he shall not be subject to the necessities which they have recognized as paramount in life. Illness, death, renunciation of enjoyment, restrictions on his own will, shall not touch him; the laws of nature and of society shall be abrogated in his favor; he shall once more really be the centre and core of creation—'His Majesty the Baby', as we once fancied ourselves. The child shall fulfill those wishful dreams of the parents which they never carried out—the boy shall become a great man and a hero in his father's place, and the girl shall marry a prince as a tardy compensation for her mother. At the most touchy point in the narcissistic system, the immortality of the ego, which is so hard pressed by reality, security is achieved by taking refuge in the child. Parental love, which is so moving and at bottom so childish, is nothing but the parents' narcissism born again, which, transformed into object-love, unmistakably reveals its former nature (1914, p. 90f.).

Does Freud's thought here go beyond what other writers have said about parents and children having a shared unconscious (e.g., Wickes, 1927, p. 35f.), or is it just a different way of saying it? In terms of the present line of argument, his formulation is quite helpful in making clear how it is that aggression that is "bound over" to the parent's superego can affect the child. If the superego of the parent depletes his own supply of narcissistic libido through destructive attack—in the way that we saw illustrated above by Amy and John—, then is there not a direct connection with the ego of the child through the shared narcissism? It would seem that whatever punitive force attacks the parent's ego has direct access to the ego of the child.

My reason for introducing this point about the shared narcissism between parent and child, with the corollary of the shared effects of superego severity in diminished self-regard in both, is to point out a seeming paradox. Is it then the case that the harder parents strive toward perfection at being parents, in their homage to their own ego ideal, the more danger there is that the tendency of aggression to turn around on itself will result in destructiveness toward the ego of the children and diminish their narcissistic supplies, the nourishment of their own self-regard?

It seems that the route I have taken through Freud's insights about the tricks that can be played by aggression on unsuspecting mortals, that is, that it can make itself felt in the guise of conscience and can turn around on the self has led only to a problem. If ambivalence, or the coexistence of aggression, both positive and negative, with libidinal feelings is not to be dispensed with through the route of high moral standards, how is it to be dealt with? If the problem of aggression, through this more hidden route, is as vicious in its potential to thwart the growth of the ego as in families at the other extreme, in families where there is insufficient control and moral responsibility, how is the child's ego, in its emerging state, to be enabled to flourish? In this light, the predicament of children like Amy and John is not so very different from that of children like William. The families of both are faced with the fundamental problem of ambivalence of feeling.

Perhaps we have come full circle now, back to the question of how it is that instinctual urges get sublimated, or transformed, as distinguished from repressed. If Freud is right that we have been fooled if we think that moralistic behavior can sublimate instinctual urges, that the aggression simply moves in on another plane—through the superego—then how it is that sublimation authentically takes place, and how it is that the parental matrix makes that sublimation possible, becomes a very important question indeed.

The children in Chapter I offered us a clue that one way to approach this question is through play. Their play provides us with a specific locus where symbolic creativity and human relationship converge, and it may be helpful—in pursuing further how these two foci are interrelated in bringing about new levels of being in the children—to investigate in greater detail this matter of play.

Chapter VII

AMBIVALENCE OF FEELING AND PLAY

In the last chapter I drew our attention to some of the facts regarding the inevitability of ambivalence in human beings in general and in the relationships between parents and children in particular. I also tried to show that the attempt to deny all negative feeling in the interest of idealism has the paradoxical effect of aggravating the destructive aggression in us all, and that the sadism of the moral agency in the parent has direct access to the ego of the child, with perhaps as much risk to the ego-needs of the child as aggression expressed more directly.

We were left with the question of whether there is some way to avoid this apparent double bind in regard to negative feelings, the question of what alternative there might be to the route of repressive idealism, as well as to the route of undercontrolled aggression. The answer to this question is clearly not to be found in the error of permissiveness, per se, in the relationships with our children. To abandon a child to his instinctual urges is quite as unloving, and indeed sadistic, as to attack the child's ego through the severity of the family moral agency. We want, rightly, our children to "behave well." Since Freud has shown us, however, that behaving well is not the same as transformed instinct (Freud, 1915, p. 281f.), it is necessary to return to the original question of this inquiry and ask again how instinctual drives—now shown to be aggressive as well as libidinal, hateful as well as loving, destructive as well as life-giving—get transformed into something new.

It has been my working hypothesis that this transformation involves symbolic creativity in the context of a relationship of a certain kind, and it is my goal to arrive at a clearer understanding of what that certain kind of relationship consists of, the qualities in it that facilitate the new creations. Before that goal can be reached, however, it is necessary to ponder further the question that has been raised about ambivalence, and what can be done with it, in recognition of the fact that repression of its negative poles does not bring us very far forward.

While there is much to be found in the literature on this subject, and I want to take advantage of some of that wealth, there is a source of insight into how ambivalence can be handled that lies closer to hand, and that rich resource is children's play.

A youngster at play, if the atmosphere is safe—and that is a part of the story to come—is not embarrassed about ambivalence. The bad guys are just as welcome to center stage as the good guys. We saw in Chapter I abundant evidence of the negative side of things: bad snakes, "that could kill us, you know," robbers, murderers, wild animals, and villains of every description came right into the action without apology.

A young patient of mine, who at seven years of age has more than her share of ambivalence to manage, stages in the playroom the most vivid enactments of badness. There is a wicked mother doll, for example, who threatens her children with death if they do not go to sleep. The child herself can turn into a barbarian and scream unquotable epithets and curses at any available target—usually at me, but sometimes at a toy—only to stop suddenly, smile at me, and say, "Don't worry, I'm only playing." When "wild things" are only play, when they are toy animals, or just word pictures of "Bang!" and "Rip!," they do not pose any difficulty for children.

What is there to be learned from watching children play in this way? No doubt there are many things to be learned, but the emphasis I want to make here is that the children have discovered spontaneously a way to handle ambivalence of feeling.

As we saw in the last chapter, aggressive and destructive feelings are present in all of us, and the question of what to do with them is critical in the development of a child into full flower. Given reasonable opportunity, the child will find ways to deal with these feelings, ways to transfer some of the battle going on *inside* to the *outside*, onto toys, onto pets, onto other people. In their play, children find, or make, representatives of the internal struggles: they cast the toys into whatever roles they please, rearrange reality according to their liking, manipulate these items in ways that enable them to work over personal concerns. When there is some anxiety threatening in the real world, play enables children to take an active part in replicating situations in which they have felt themselves to be passive victims.[1]

No doubt this conversion of the passive role into the active one, so critical in the ego's growth to its full stature, is the reason that girls like to play mother and that all children love to play school and take the teacher role; that a gift of magic tricks is so sure to please a youngster, who so frequently feels the inequity of power distribution in the family and thus takes delight in some omnipotent reversal of this inequality. In play—at least until an age when the world, alas, will no longer allow it—a child may place his own unacceptable parts onto an imaginary playmate, thus creating a whipping boy, of a sort, to bear the bad impulses, or, conversely, may create an idealized companion who receives all the infinite adulation and satisfaction that the child feels denied in the real world, or companions to serve any purpose at all in the service of the child (Wickes, 1927, p. 156f.).

Since the specific focus of the present discussion is the relevance of play to the problem of ambivalence, I want to return to those "bad guys," mentioned above, and investigate further their identity. The assumption is that they represent, in the main, the child's own aggression, though, as we have seen in the last chapter, they also have reference to figures in the outside world. One question that comes to mind in connection with these ubiquitous bad guys is why they are so bad. Why is there such fantastic exaggeration of the badness of the villains, exaggeration that has its corollary, of course, in the goodness of the other extreme, such that of fairy god-mothers.

This question could be illumined from several theoretical perspectives, most fruitfully, perhaps, from the viewpoint of Jung. The

---

[1] For a classic statement of the psychoanalytic theory of play, which addresses such issues as mastery, wish-fulfillment, and repetition, see Wälder, 1932.

exaggeration could be explained as the coalescence of subjective reactions, external realities, and the mythical and cultural heritage of the ages that make up our mental images of significant people in our lives, as described, for example, under the concept of *imago*:

> The imago combines object and subject reactions to the object, conscious experience, and the influence of unconscious archetypes into a symbolic image representing the meeting of all these levels of reality (Ulanov, 1975, p. 225).

We have only to reflect a moment on the exaggerated qualities of the figures of fairy-tale and folklore to grasp the fact that the images of good and bad in the human psyche are more gigantic than the everyday world would in general warrant (Von Franz, 1970; Bettelheim, 1976).

Melanie Klein makes the matter of these exaggerated figures in the minds of children quite clear, from her point of view, and I want to consider for a moment her thought about their identity. It was mentioned above that for Klein children's internalized objects are in no wise synonymous with the actual, external parent from which they derived. The child's internal object is, no doubt, a coalescence of instinctual urges, colored-lens perception of the parental handling, and a unique appropriation and elaboration of the primordial and cultural heritage in the human mind,[2] as truly as it is an identification with the actual parent. Klein explains that the reason the bad guys are so bad, the internal images so frightening and so ferocious, is that they represent the child's own pregenital impulses:

> The imagos adopted in this early phase of ego-development bear the stamp of the pregenital instinctual impulses, although they are actually constructed on the basis of the real Oedipus objects. These early levels are responsible for the phantastic imagos which devour, cut to pieces, and overpower...(1929b, p. 204).

In simple terms, there are in every child's development stages in which oral sadism and anal sadism, in Freudian theory, make up a part

---

[2] While the primordial heritage of the mind is more commonly associated with the thought of Jung, Freud also referred to it. In the last lines of the *Outline of Psycho-Analysis*, written shortly before his death, Freud spoke of the significance of primeval phylogenetic experience (1940, p. 206f.).

of the normal order of things. Instinctual urges, which loom large relative to the underdeveloped young ego, become engaged in conflict with the imagos of the parent, which are also exaggerated, as we have seen, and this is a great deal for the inner world of a child to manage. In the small world of toys and dolls, children find ways to project some of this battle to the outside, and this world offers the possibility of enormous relief from the inner conflicts (Klein, 1955, p. 138).

Klein provides us with a most entertaining example of the extravagant dimensions of the inner warfare between a little boy's own impulses and the maternal imago, projected onto the outside world. This scene is taken from a Ravel opera, which was being revived in Vienna at the time Klein was writing her article.

The mother has just given the little boy some admonition, and the following is presented on stage:

> The child flies into a rage. He jumps up, drums on the door, sweeps the teapot and cup from the table, so that they are broken into a thousand pieces. He climbs onto the window-seat, opens the cage and tries to stab the squirrel with his pen....The child jumps down from the window and seizes the cat. He yells and swings the tongs, pokes the fire furiously in the open grate, and with his hands and feet hurls the kettle into the room. A cloud of ashes and steam escapes. He swings the tongs like a sword and begins to tear the wall paper. Then he opens the case of the grand-father clock and snatches out the copper pendulum. He pours the ink over the table. Exercise books and other books fly through the air. Hurrah!...
>
> The things he has maltreated come to life. An armchair refused to let him sit in it or have the cushions to sleep on. Table, chair, bench and sofa suddenly lift up their arms and cry: 'Away with the dirty little creature!' The clock has a dreadful stomach-ache and begins to strike the hours like mad. The tea-pot leans over the cup, and they begin to talk Chinese....The stove spits out a shower of sparks at him....From under the cover of a book...there emerges a little old man....He is the spirit of mathematics, and begins to put the child through an examination: millimetre, centimetre, barometer, trillion—eight and eight are forty....The child falls down in a faint! (1929a, p. 210f.).

This passage is quoted here because it expresses so vividly the magnified quality of the battle between a child's instinctual urges and the parental imago and the way in which projection is used to externalize the battle. The maltreated things begin to live. There is an interpenetration between the inner world and the outer world that requires of the child some way to sort it all out, and that way is the opportunity to play. In play, anything goes: the scene doesn't have to be ethical, logical, integrated, or even coherent; play can be any way at all; it can, in effect, transcend the conflict.

Children are enormously resourceful in finding ways to externalize these urgent matters in the inner world, as we have been shown by Amy, John, and William. The most difficult feelings can be managed when some bearer in the outside world can be found to represent and depict them. Amy's little dolls, who lived all those months in a bottom drawer, enabled Amy to share her burdens and her joys with them in such a way that her own anxieties and fears and guilt feelings were reduced, and the heavy task of keeping these feelings repressed was alleviated. In addition, she was able to discover new things in herself through these dolls, for example, her own reasons for giving up her excessive withdrawal into books: "After all," she said, "they can't read all the time; I'm going to let them play with the animals instead."

Klein offers a number of very interesting examples of the ways in which she, as therapist, was assigned various roles by young patients in the interest of externalization (1929b, p. 199f.). At one point, she would represent the child's severe superego and was required to pretend harshness; at another, she would be assigned the role of the child, in which role she had to have inflicted upon her imagined tortures and humiliations.

A young patient, who was referred to me because her behavior belied more intense instinctual pressures, in terms of destructive urges, and more sadism from the superego than she could sustain in reality, began to have less need for psychotic defenses when she was able to externalize some of the inner difficulties. Sometimes she would tell me I had been very, very bad and would play locking me in jail. Sometimes she would go to the toy phone and report all my wicked deeds to the police in most colorful language. Over and over she would yell "Shut Up!" to me when I was already silent, in an attempt to quiet her own raging signals inside. What seemed to help her most at these times was to pretend to tape my mouth closed until she was more confident of being able to control her own inner riot. At other times, she would switch roles back and forth with me, trying first the naughty child part, then the correcting parent part, and then back again. I would be instructed at times to "cry, and cry, and cry, and keep crying," so that she could be the comforting mother who would pat my head and assure me things were going to be all right.

To sum up what Klein has contributed to our understanding of children's play: In her view, children are able to project their inner conflicts between impulse and parental image and thus to manage in this way some of the aggression from their own instinctual urges and the aggression from the superego. They handle the problem of ambivalence of feeling by externalizing it in such a way as to be able to work it over and thereby gain relief from the anxiety.

From this point of view, Amy, John, and William were using caterpillars, and wild animals, and soldiers, and cars, and bird cages, and mountain hideouts for dramatic enactment through fantasy images of their own conflicting impulses—and eventually of the resolutions they found. They were also, from Klein's perspective, accomplishing something else: they were altering the frightening, ferocious quality of their own internal objects by the appropriation of the transference relationship to the therapist (Klein, 1950, p. 47). It will be the task of the next chapter to explore what the qualities in that transference relationship might be that make possible this alteration in the frightening qualities of the old objects, this modification, in Freudian terms, of the severity of the superego. At the present juncture, however, it is the child's use of play per se in gaining mastery over ambivalence that I mean to underline.

The notion of mastery over the various areas of life through play brings us in the natural course of things to Erik Erikson, who stressed particularly the role of play in ego-mastery:

> Play, then, is a function of the ego, an attempt to synchronize the bodily and social processes with the self....Yet the emphasis, I think, should be on the ego's need to master the various areas of life, and especially those in which the individual finds his self, his body, and his social role wanting and trailing (Erikson, 1950, p. 211f.).

Erikson's contribution to our understanding of play has been enormous, not only in the clinical, but also in the developmental, social, and philosophical spheres. His observations about play illumine a wide range of human experience, from the earliest interplay between mother and infant, through the whole gamut of psychosocial development in childhood, adolescence, and adulthood, and his insights about play extend into the social and political arena (1950, 1959, 1972, 1977). To do justice to Erikson's thought on play would in itself be a worthy project.

In the present connection, it is Erikson's recent emphasis on certain kinds of play as having the role in human life of *managing ambivalence* that seems most pertinent—that is, *ritualized* play.

Erikson observes that the inevitable presence of aggression in all living calls for a *"creative formalization,* which helps to avoid both *impulsive* excess and *compulsive* self-restriction, both social anomie and moralistic coercion" (Erikson, 1977, p. 82). [Italics his.]

Because Erikson's observations about how aggression and ambivalence are addressed in ritual are relevant to the line of thought I am pursuing about the handling of these emotional facts in parent-child relationship, I want to provide here a thought provoking passage:

> A fundamental and almost innocent "aggressivity" informs every act of being alive—and thus of being playful. It simply belongs to a growing organism's very existence in space and time—and, indeed, *aggredere* means first and foremost to *go at* things and people in a way that may invites playful mutuality but may also interfere with their leeway without being antagonistic in either intention or affect. I call it "almost innocent," however, because in man acts of reciprocal interference soon lead to experiences of frustration and rage, shame and guilt. For it is a basic fact of human existence that, while the individual needs leeway in order to grow and to develop, he must from the start learn to limit his aggression by absorbing into his behavior and by taking into his conscience the mores of the cultural setting, which, lacking the animal's instinctive embeddedness in a segment of nature, must provide boundaries and rules of interplay as well as a total world view promising some leeway for all as well as some sanctioned ways of usurpation for some (Erikson, 1977, p. 56f). [Italics his.]

Erikson goes on to say that it is mutual interplay, beginning in the earliest reciprocity between mother and infant, "which counteracts in childhood as it alleviates in later life the human readiness for bewildered reaction and rage" (p. 57), and that "the great human gift of *ritualization* adds structure and predictability" to the vital encounters of interplay between human beings. He sees "games, in childhood and beyond, as a most basic and inventive form of interplay on the border of affiliative and antagonistic interaction" (p. 58).

As usual, Erikson's pregnant thought is encased in enigmatic and abbreviated terms, and I do not want to miss what he is saying here.

Throughout this series of lectures, of which this book consists, Erikson is concerned with this matter of ritualization, which he distinguishes from the pathological meaning of the word:

> When in psychopathology we speak of an individual's "handwashing ritual," we mean that he scrubs his hands, in tortured solitude, until they become raw, and yet he never feels clean. But this blatantly contradicts the anthropological meaning of the word, which assigns to "ritual" a deepened communality, a proven ceremonial form, a timeless quality from which all participants emerge with a sense of awe and purification (Erikson, 1977, p. 78).

Erikson's phrase above, "interplay on the border of affiliative and antagonistic interaction" suggests what it is that I am seeking here—that is, what do parents and children, who are so closely "affiliated," do with their antagonisms, in light of the fact that denying them is not a helpful way out? Erikson suggests that throughout the life cycle, beginning with the way a mother comes predictably to approach her infant in a kind of ritual of daily care, there are certain means by which persons learn to deal with these ambiguities, ways that are built from the beginning on a "mutuality of recognition":

> There is much to suggest that man is born with the need for such regular and mutual affirmation and certification: we know at any rate that its absence can harm an infant radically, by diminishing or extinguishing his search for impressions which will verify his senses. This need will reassert itself in every stage of life as a demand for ever new, ever more formalized and more widely shared ritualizations (and, eventually, rituals) which repeat the face-to-face "recognition" and the name-to-name correspondence of the hoped for. Such ritualizations range from the regular exchange of greeting affirming a strong emotional bond, to tradition greetings affirming a reciprocity of roles, to singular encounters in love or inspiration, and, eventually, in a leader's "charisma" as confirmed by (more or less) exquisite statues and paintings, or by mere multiplied banners and televised appearances. All such meetings at their best embody seeming paradoxes: they are *playful* and yet *formalized*: quite *familiar* through repetition, they yet renew the *surprise* of recognition. And while the ethnologists will tell us that ritualizations in the animal world must, above all, be unambiguous sets of signals.., we suspect that in man the overcoming of *ambivalence* (as well as of ambiguity) is one of the prime functions of ritualization. For as we love our children, and children in general, they can also arouse hate and murderous disdain, even as at best they will find us arbitrary in rejection and possessive in acceptance, if not

potentially dangerous and witchlike. What we love or admire is always threatening; awe becomes awfulness, and benevolence harbors the danger of being consumed by wrath. Therefore, ritualized affirmation, reaching from daily life to religious rites, becomes indispensable as a periodical experience and must in changing times find new and meaningful forms (1977, p. 88f.). [Italics his.]

While Erikson goes on to apply this perspective not only to games and competitive sports but to the wider arena of international political realities, the relevance of his comments for our purpose has to do with these matters of mutual recognition expressed in, and confirmed by, ways in which families have of responding to each other, including play.

Erikson confirms what has been attested by Freud, Klein, and others that murderous, as well as loving, feelings pervade all human relationship, and that we ignore this fact to our peril. He points out, in passing, that in animals the interruption of ritualized behavior "by which animals do away with ambiguity can lead to murder" (1972, p. 142), and the import of that observation would of course be that there may be analogous danger in the human community in the absence of adequate means to deal with ambivalence.

Klein, then, has emphasized the role of play in externalizing inner conflict, and Erikson, adding to that emphasis—which he too has frequently made—has drawn our attention to the role of playful and formalized ways of mutual recognition in handling ambivalence. To push the question of play further, it would seem that play offers two alternative routes, somewhat analogous to each other, but with some clear differences: one route being that of games and competitive sports, and the other, the route of symbolic creativity.

Adrian Stokes, mentioned above, has written with great insight about some of the psychoanalytic implication of ball games (1973b). He addresses the question of differences in organized games and art, including: the greater proportion of the aggressive relative to the libidinal in the former; the toleration for crudity, and even ugliness, in athletic sports; and the large element of luck essential to the wide appeal of competitive games.

> In tune with the healthy catharsis of aggression implicit in organized games, some reserved or even pretentious kinds of ugliness, an external

moderate manifestation of aggression, of the unconverted sense of destruction, as well as a share in beauty, seem to be not only well tolerated, but actively needed by the ordinary man under modern conditions. Moreover, I think that as well as avoiding art, modern team games can serve as a substitute for it, being in some ways a parallel re-creation, though composed largely of a crude genital sublimation that ignores the sustained feminine receptivity whose collaboration is needed for aesthetic experience. Games must dramatize the unrhythmic chanciness of reality: a large element of luck is essential to their wide appeal: the player makes trial of his good fortune as well as of his skill; he is "chancing his hand," his potency and his power to compel (Stokes, 1973b, p. 40).

Stokes, following Helene Deutsch (1926), points in this article to a much wider inclusion in competitive ball games, however, of the whole gamut of libidinal, as well as aggressive, components than has been generally recognized—including oral as well as the more transparent genital content. He mentions, for example, the "repeated endurance of symbolic castration...and the power thereupon sometimes developed...to resurrect the sense of potency after smashing defeat...." (p. 39). Commenting further on the genital content, he says:

> Our games serve to reflect the emotional alternations which are typical of the adolescent in the process of controlling and directing the rush of genital feelings; the quick change, for instance, from active to passive, from attack to defense, from feeling of omnipotence to those of lurid disaster. They reflect also the huge patience to be learned in our civilisation for the attainment of propitious genital satisfaction....A very valuable feature, all will agree, is the catharsis in modern games—it is more a catharsis than a sublimation—of aggression, controlled by the super-ego and harmonised with the libidinal content. To be any good one must freely want to smack the ball (1973b, p. 41).

Stokes goes on to clarify the oedipal content of ball games, with their winning and losing of "home," the "race of occupy the hole," and spatial analogies to the oedipal contest over the mother's body.

I mention this article of Stokes in order to point to the fact that there is an entire avenue of approach to the question of play and ambivalence—the route of sports and athletics—that lies in a direction quite different from the route I have elected to take. It is not to devalue this route, but rather to follow the path dictated by the therapeutic journeys, that I leave the approach of competitive games to another investigator, as interesting as it is to ponder, especially in connection with Erikson's emphasis on ritualized mutual recognition as related to the overcoming of ambivalence. Competitive games would certainly be an example of such ritualization "on the border of affiliative and antagonistic interaction" (Erikson, 1977, p. 58).

I will stay, then, with this pursuit of the handling of ambivalence in the direction of play as symbolic creativity, the approach that was spelled out especially in Ricoeur's elaboration of Freud's idea of sublimation (Chapter II), that is, play as forming a part of a continuum that includes poetry and art, and as being a part of the "oneiric mask," all that is hidden and veiled in human experience, all that is analogous to the dream.

The children's journeys were examples of this oneiric mask, and I want to stay close to the original question as to how their symbolic creativity, and the relational context in which it occurred, are related to the therapeutic changes that were observed. In pursuing this question, I have traversed a route through the classical frameworks of Freud and Jung, finding in both of them a connection between symbolic creativity and human relationship; through an exploration of the beginnings of symbol formation in the first human bond, that with the mother; through an investigation of relationship between parents and children as the context for personality development in general and for symbolization and sublimation in particular; and through some of the implications of the meeting of ego-needs of children, in Winnicott's terms. Meeting of ego-needs includes the necessity of recognizing and dealing with ambivalence of feeling in the family, a necessity that is not met by the route of moral idealism and repression. The present focus has been on how the arena of play might offer an alternative route to repression as a way of handling ambivalence and of meeting the need of the child's ego to come forth into its own stature.

Each of the children in Chapter I shared with us a journey that carved out for the child an alternate route to repression. Take, for example, Amy's image of the large, red doghouse. She had placed this doghouse far from the house where she lived, apparently to express her own isolation from her impulse life.

How did she use this creation to find her way out of the problem? She began by casting the problem in an image, as one might do in a dream, that expressed the concern, that is, the doghouse. Then she began to play with this doghouse. She considered aloud whether she should bring a little toy dog from home to occupy this dwelling, and arrived the next week with the dog. Then she thought further about it and came the following week with those wriggly caterpillars in a covered jar. She had found something in the outside world that represented something in her inside world, namely certain impulses that she felt she had to keep under tight control. In the safety of the containing relationship, she was then able to give a try—in miniature—to the experiment of "letting them play a little." The caterpillars, managed adroitly by the paper-doll mother and little girl, were made at first to occupy the doghouse, but were then allowed to come outside and play on the swing.

What Amy was doing was taking the problem itself—the isolated impulse life—and finding a way to give it dramatic rendition[3] in such a way that her play with the images worked out her own resolution. The playing of the caterpillars on the swing, and the playing of her little mice on the grass, and her dolphin playing in the water fulfilled her own prophecy in regard to the liberated life she was bringing forth: "There are going to be others!", she had said. Others there were, both in the playroom and in the larger world, to which she was able to take the new stirrings of life within herself and let them breathe. We see here a confirmation of the lines of Hölderlin, to which Jungians often refer (e.g., Edinger, 1972, p. 37),

> Wo aber Gefahr ist
> wächst das Rettende auch.
>
> (Where danger lies,
> Grows the solution nearby.)

In drawing together these various threads on the subject of play, I want to come back to Winnicott at this point, because his particular theory of play may offer the most direct route to the goal I am seeking, that is, to understand how the children's symbolic creativity and the

---

[3] Loewald (1975) considers the psychoanalytic situation as a drama that re-enacts a previous action. In this discussion of "Psychoanalysis as an Art and the Fantasy Character of the Psychoanalytic Situation," he builds on Aristotle's definition of tragedy as "the imitation of action in the form of action." Psychoanalysis as drama would extend the point made here about Amy into the sphere of adult psychoanalysis, that is, working out a problem through dramatic rendition in the transference.

containing relationship were related to the personality growth in the children.

In Chapter III, in connection with the question of how the use of symbol begins in infancy, I referred to Winnicott's special contribution in exploring an area between the private, intrapsychic world and the world of external reality shared with others. This in-between space, says Winnicott, is observable in the phenomenon of the transitional object—the teddy, or the scrap of blanket, or whatever article in the baby's experience is used in a special way—that is, as something that is invested with the baby's own psychic energy and also that of the mother. It is not just "subjective," nor is it just "objective," but it shares qualities of both. It is "on the way" in baby's journeying from inside to outside, and it marks the beginning of an intermediate space between the two, the area of play and of experiencing, the "place where we live" (1971, Chaps 1, 5, 7, 8).

It was also mentioned above that the transitional object, this first rudimentary symbol, is born out of the paradox that the baby creates or hallucinates something that coincides with the mother's timely provision of the world of real events, that is, the breast. As we have seen in Chapter V, this successful first "creation" depends for its success on the "nearly 100% adjustment of the mother" (Winnicott, 1971), to the needs of her infant, at first, in order for the baby to have the experience of illusory omnipotence over the breast, which Winnicott understands to be the root of creativity.

There has to be a holding environment, explored above in some detail, for the infant's needs to be met in terms of the ego. In addition to the provision for the experience of illusion, it is the function of the mother in the holding environment to provide gradual "disillusionment," that is, the finely graduated impingement of reality. Because other pressing matters come along that require mother's attention, she, of necessity, allows the infant recognition that the baby is not omnipotent, and that she cannot magically fulfill his every wish. Indeed, if she could fulfill all the baby's wishes magically, she would be a witch, a magician, who cannot be trusted (Winnicott, 1960, p. 52).

I review this thought of Winnicott's as background for making clearer how Winnicott's view of *play* differs from those dealt with above, that is, Klein and Erikson. For Winnicott, the point of play is not primarily a pragmatic matter of handling instinctual tension.

Instinctual tension belongs, says Winnicott, to the intrapsychic sphere, and for him play is not simply a traffic interchange between inner and outer, a place where the inner tensions can be put on the outside and then worked over, as Klein saw it to be.

For Winnicott, play is something in its own right; it is its own end; it is the beginning of a place where we live, where the true self emerges and finds expression, as opposed to the "false self" that can be built up on the basis of compliance only. When the requirements of the outside world serve as substitute for the child's own spontaneous gesture—and this substitution can begin in the very first feeding situation—or, when instinctual tension on the inside takes over the child's world, then there is no play. Play belongs to a sphere that is neither a matter of instinctual gratification and discharge nor a matter of external reality; it is a sphere the ego has for its own gratification and its own unfolding:

> It is in playing and only in playing that the individual child or adult is able to be creative and to use the whole personality, and it is only in being creative that the individual discovers the self (Winnicott, 1971, p. 54).

As we have seen earlier, the significance of the play space in the life of the infant, for Winnicott, is extended from the space of the first transitional object into all those areas of life where "illusion is allowed," that is, where there is not a strict conformity to verifiable accuracy, namely those areas of art, religion, philosophy, and creative work of all kinds:

> This intermediate area of experience, unchallenged in respect of its belonging to inner or external (shared) reality, constitutes the greater part of the infant's experience, and throughout life is retained in the intense experiencing that belongs to the arts and to religion and to imaginative living, and to creative scientific work (Winnicott, 1971, p. 14).

Thus, for Winnicott, play, beginning in the transitional space between baby and the first outside work, namely mother, and growing out of the overlap of baby's first "illusion" with the "something really provided out there," that is, the breast, becomes diffused over all later experiences of shared play spaces and cultural experience, and, in short, *life* as we experience it. It is not a matter, says Winnicott, of illness or health; it is a matter of *what life is about* (Winnicott, 1971, p. 100).

What do these different theories of play offer to our understanding of how Amy was able to use her dog house, in the contained space with the therapist, to come into her own new dimensions of life, how John was able to experiment with ways of taking his power with him instead of leaving it behind, how William found the courage to try a new street?

I mentioned above that, from Klein's viewpoint, the children could be understood, not only to be externalizing their inner conflicts onto the outside world, but to be altering the ferociousness of the parental imago by the appropriation of a new relationship in the transference to the therapist (Klein, 1950, p. 47). In Winnicott's view, there is a shift of accent, namely that it is the holding object which makes possible the play, and it is the play itself, the experience of being creative, that is the thing that life is about.[4] How might these two points of view be integrated in such a way as to shed light on my question?

I believe that both Winnicott and Klein are right. The object relationship makes possible the symbolic play, as Winnicott sees it, and the symbolic play is an opportunity, as Klein explains it, to externalize conflicts and to alter the ferocious qualities of the old objects and the ego's own situation, that is, the predominance of the good inside over the bad.

My own way of conceptualizing how the children's symbolic play and the relationship are connected, in addition to the insights of Klein and Winnicott, is that the children through their play were, in the simplest terms, "eating" the therapist. That is to say, they were appropriating, through *participating via the symbol* in a vital force present in the containing relationship. Of course what the children internalized, or "ate," to use the simple image, was not synonymous with the person of the therapist, any more than the old internal objects were replicas of the actual parents. It was, to use Klein's term, *fantasy*. However, I am convinced that there are certain qualities in the therapeutic relationship that make possible the arousing of the creative urge in the child, the mobilizing of that individual's own vital force in bringing forth

---

[4] A view of play that would seem to be congenial with Winnicott's, and one that also finds itself in opposition to the conflict model of Klein, is *In Praise of Play* by Robert Neale. Neale sees play as an expression of inner harmony and defines it as *"any activity not motivated by the need to resolve inner conflict"* (Neale, 1969, p. 24). Neale's view is also in keeping with that mentioned by Erikson (1977), namely Plato's view: "He sees the model of true playfulness in the need of all young creatures, animal and human to leap (Erikson, 1977, p. 17). [Italics mine.]

what had lain dormant. There is some power at work, a power that makes possible the alteration of ferocity in old objects, but also makes possible the children's discovery of possibilities in themselves of which they were previously unaware.

The child, mentioned above, who showed me how strong his arm muscle was growing "because of the tea" expressed more clearly than any explanation my point of emphasis: As the child "eats" the parent—or therapist—or teacher, the child gets fatter. Just as the nourishment is appropriated through symbolic elements, such as William's dough and cake, new levels of being within the self are also expressed through symbolic creations, which speak their own messages of enlargement more completely than any interpretation of them. To borrow again the words of Gaston Bachelard,

> The poetic image is under the sign of a new being. This new being is happy man" (1958, p. xxv).

Amy's expanding snail that crept into her pictures; the horned, mighty spirit that was coming to John's house; William's new street—these were renditions of "stronger arm muscles because of the tea."

These stronger muscles, I have suggested, involved the appropriation of some power made available to the children in their nourishment in the containing relationship. It will be the task of the next chapter to explore what the nature of that power might be, what qualities it manifests, and a point of view as to the source of the power.

Chapter VIII

A THEOLOGICAL PERSPECTIVE

What about this word "power," which was introduced at the end of the last chapter? Amy, John, and William, I asserted, were able to participate, through the symbolic activity, in some power made available to them in the containing relationship, and that this vital force kindled a movement of fluorescence in the children.

Freud would have called this power transference, and Jung would have added something to the notion of transference, probably along the lines of connection to the Self. I would agree that both of these formulations provide a great deal of insight into the nature of the power.

However, there is in my view still something mysterious about this force in the transference relationship. We know, of course, that it involves a shifting of libido, both intrapsychically and interpersonally with a new object, and we know a great deal about the kind of situation that facilitates this transference (Greenson, 1965, p. 111; Horney, 1963, p. 155; Macalpine, 1950, p. 519; Racker, 1968). It is the maximal use of this knowledge about how to elicit and harness transference that lies at the core of classical psychoanalysis and its modifications.

It would be generally agreed that there are certain qualities of relationship that are the *sine qua non* of a good transference in any school of psychotherapy, and I have already stated above that there is considerable weight of opinion that these are the same qualities that are necessary for the nurturance of the young ego in the parent-child relationship. While this premise is not, of course, a scientific fact, it is an assumption widely shared by psychoanalysts, including such writers as Klein, Winnicott, and Harold Searles, who move back and forth from the parent-child to the therapeutic relationship in such a way as to make clear that they believe these to be different manifestations of the same kind of human situation. Modell (1976, p. 291) has referred to the different viewpoints as to whether psychoanalytic therapy is or is not a recapitulation of the early relationship with the mother, and, while that claim is somewhat stronger than a statement of paradigmatic comparison, it is a related question.

Medard Boss, an Existentialist, has stated that the qualities required in the therapeutic relationship differ from and surpass those of the parental one and, in fact, that these qualities are unique to psychotherapy:

> This 'psychotherapeutic eros' is different from the love of parents for their children, different from the love between two friends, different from the love of the priest for his flock, decidedly different from the extremely variable love between the sexes, and different from the matter-of-fact indifference of purely conventional kindness. Genuine psychotherapeutic eros, in other words, must be an otherwise never-practiced selflessness, self-restraint, and reverence before the partner's existence and uniqueness. These qualities must not be shaken or perturbed by cooperative, indifferent, or hostile behavior on the part of the patient. Psychotherapeutic eros must go beyond even Christian humility in its selflessness, its modesty, and its triumph over egotism, in that it must not intervene even in the interest of the therapist's own God to seek to guide the partner's life (1963, p. 259f.).

These words from Boss raise an important question: Where do these stunning qualities of "never-practiced selflessness, self-restraint, and reverence before the partner's existence and uniqueness" come from? How does one attain them? Presumably, if one is so fortunate as to be able to exercise such noble attributes, he has come across them elsewhere, and that elsewhere, it would be generally agreed, is in the original bond with the parent or in some later profound tie with a parent figure who provided them. "What have ye that ye did not receive?" asked Paul, the apostle.

Therefore, we arrive again at the question, what are the qualities in good parents that make it possible for the personality of the child to develop optimally, or—to state the question in the specific terms already used—to enable the child to transform instinctual drives in a forward direction toward maturation, toward one's full stature? Can these qualities be identified, and, if so, from what source do they derive?

The qualities Boss speaks of as belonging to psychotherapeutic eros, which in no wise could be attained unless one had experienced these attributes in abundance in his own personal ties, cannot, in fact, be so simply accounted for. They are somewhat mysterious, I am suggesting, in their origins. That they are learned from parents tells us something, but it doesn't tell us enough. Freud would no doubt have identified them as deriving from Eros, or the Life instinct; Jung would see them as a manifestation of the God archetype, or the Self, in the human psyche. A different point of view as to their origins has been suggested to me by the theologian, Karl Barth, and it is his perspective that recommends itself as the framework for my inquiry into the specific qualities of relationship toward which I have been groping above.

If I were to state what I understand to be the most significant, lasting contribution of Karl Barth, it would be his point of departure in the attempt to enlighten the human condition. Barth was convinced that no anthropological perspective is useful as a starting point for understanding who we are. The human subject, in Barth's view, can be understood only by the light of God's own revealing of Himself. In effect, Barth reverses the usual procedure for thinking about God and humanity, which is to begin with human experience, to identify something that seems good, to project this idea of goodness to an ultimate dimension and call it "God."

Barth says that this point of departure will never result in our knowing anything about God, nor furthermore, in knowing anything about ourselves. If we begin with human considerations and proceed on a line upward toward the highest and best that we know, we are dealing with the projection of our own image, the divinizing of some cultural pattern or our own inner experience.

Barth insists that the arrow points in the other direction, that the human subject and the human action are enlightened only from God's side. He asserts that we first know the love of God, then define the human action, that the knowledge of God tells us who we are. He posits that the creature can achieve self-understanding only in the context of God's love, that the possibilities of our consciousness lie in the movement of God toward us. God is not subject to our generalities, as though He were one of a species, subject to evaluation along our self-conceived lines. Rather, God informs those generalities, from his side and by his own initiative—not in concepts or philosophical abstractions, but in his giving Himself to us in ways that make Him known to us, and, derivatively, make ourselves and our idols known also.

In effect, Barth held that religion, or the creature's timeless attempt to make God into "the substance of the highest that he himself can see, choose, create, and be" (Barth, 1957, p. 168) to be quite as self-deceptive as Freud held it to be. Freud's view that the religious phenomenon arises from wish-fulfilling fantasies regarding the human need for protection against the forces of nature and the need to placate an omnipotent parent figure (e.g., 1907, 1913b, 1927), that it parallels essentially an obsessive-compulsive symptomology in its attempt to alleviate neurotic guilt feelings, is actually not far from Barth's view of religious activity: it is the divinizing of the human being's own image.

If, according to Barth, we cannot learn about ourselves or God by starting with human considerations, even the highest and best that we know, where, then, can we be enlightened? Barth says that we begin with the fact that there is a congregation praising God, and we ask, "Why?" We make our point of departure the witness of the Scripture and the Church through the ages. Why this praise?

It is the human task, says Barth, always to address itself to listening and to the attempt to comprehend anew what this age-old witness says. While he acknowledges that our understanding is always limited, ever subject to error—including his own thoughts and interpretations—, nevertheless, it is the task to keep standing under the Word as it has been passed down to us, to keep pointing to it, bearing witness to it, being corrected by it. His own image of speaking about God's self-disclosure as being analogous to walking round and round the base of a mountain and looking up at the unreachable heights from different limited perspectives is in keeping with his view of bearing witness.

To begin with our own highest and best is to subject God to our own point of view, to prefer our own moral activity to placing ourselves in a position of receiving what God offers to us; in a word, it puts ourselves above God into a position of pre-eminence, which has always, according to Scripture, been congenial to the human way of thinking. Beginning with any human perspective, either good news or bad news, and attempting to get to God that way, says Barth, will always end up in idolatry because the point of departure is a denial of the secondary position of human beings. It is our wanting to be God.

I want to accept, for the purpose of investigating effectual qualities of relationship in the parent-child, therapist-patient relationship, Barth's perspective as an arbitrary premise and see where it might lead. If we begin, as he suggests, with the praising congregation, with the witness of Scripture and the Church through the ages as to God's ways of relating to human beings as a paradigm for understanding the ways of parents with children and therapists with patients, what can we learn? If we follow Barth's summons to "think God's thoughts after him," what thoughts can come to us in the present inquiry?

An ancient Psalmist wrote about Jahweh:

> The Lord our God is merciful
> And He is gracious,
> Longsuffering, and slow to wrath,
> In mercy plenteous.
> He will not chide continually,
> Nor keep his anger still.
> With us he dealt not as we sinn'd
> Nor did requite our ill.
> 			(Psalm 103, Scottish Psalter)

This poetic encapsulation of certain qualities experienced by Israel as characteristic of Jahweh bears witness to the same attributes of God seen by other Biblical writers, both in the Hebrew Scriptures and the New Testament. Among the many ways that one can talk about the Bible, that is, as books of history, of literature, of theology, one way to see it is as books about relationship. If it were not for the danger of imposing a much later viewpoint onto an earlier one, it might be said that it is a book about object relationship. It is an account, from many sources, of the ways in which God, as parent, has been understood to relate to human beings.

Barth has conceptualized the collective witness of the Bible and the Church in some dialectic statements about the qualities of God's loving

(1957, Vol. II/1). The statements are dialectic because, as will be seen, each quality is paired in the statements with a polar opposite, which Barth sees as necessary to point to God's acting and moving in ways that are not graspable as concept, idea, or abstraction. God discloses Himself as Act, as Event, as Happening, as Subject, as Who as distinguished from What, and we can know God only as receivers of a Love that loves us first. Because we cannot possess God, we cannot know him by any philosophical epistemology; since God both reveals and hides Himself from us, as we experience it, we feel a yes and a no, a love and a wrath. It is for this reason that Barth points to God's inconceivable "perfections" through the use of dialectic statements, which also are only our necessary attempts to perceive his love. Barth makes clear that these attempts are of course not the same thing as "God."

God is seen as the very prototype of relationship and fellowship as God's own way of being—as attested in the doctrine of the Trinity—, and Barth developed this idea at length (e.g., Vol.III/4, p. 117). For the present purpose, it his exploration of what I call "the ways of God's loving" that concerns us, in order to see whether we can derive something from this approach to shed light on the human side of things that are in question in this essay.

Barth made, then, three dialectical statements about God as the One Who Loves in Freedom: he spoke of *The Grace and Holiness of God*; *The Mercy and Righteousness of God*; and *The Patience and Wisdom of God*. What does Barth mean by these words? Taking them up one at a time, let us see what they offer us.

The Grace and Holiness of God

Grace

> Grace is the distinctive mode of God's being in so far as it seeks and creates fellowship by its own free inclination and favor, unconditioned by any merit or claim in the beloved, but also unhindered by any unworthiness or opposition in the latter—able, on the contrary, to overcome all unworthiness and opposition (1957, p. 353).

Barth develops this thought of grace as God's distinct mode of relating, of turning toward human beings by his own free initiative, unconditioned by negative or positive behaviors on the part of the creature, in the gift of Himself in fellowship. Emphasis is made that this turning is not in equality, but in inequality, from one in a prior and superior position to another who has no claim at all on this condescension. He owes nothing to any counterpart.

> His inclination, good will and favour which He turns toward His partner in this act of condescension is a sheer gift which something necessarily called forth by it can neither precede not follow, for whatever follows it has its ground in this prevenient cause. It is thus a gift in this strictest sense of the term (p. 355).

There are four accents that Barth places on the nature of grace that may be particularly enlightening in the present context:

> It cannot be earned. It is conditioned by no meritorious action on the part of the receiver.
>
> It is unhindered by unworthiness or opposition.
>
> Grace precedes law, not vice-versa.
>
> Grace is inherently powerful and overcomes enmity against it without violating the self-determination of those in the grips of the enmity.

The cannot-earn quality of grace. This aspect of grace, which is a central theme of the New Testament, is a scandal, an offense to our ordinary way of thinking. We have an innate resistance to it that Barth would say is directly commensurate with our preference for our own moral activity to a gift of grace, that is, our idolatry. The idea of a prior, uncontingent, prevenient moving toward another, independent of the other's deserving, grates on our sense of justice. We are conditioned to think in terms of reward and punishment, consequences, *quid-pro-quo.* One earns what one gets; one reaps what one sows. To reverse the order, to suggest acceptance unconditioned by merit, is assaultive, not only to the work ethic by which adult responsibility is encouraged, but to our understanding of cause and effect. It is assaultive also to the *lex taliones* that is primordial in its history and immortal in the unconscious; wrong doing throws something out of kilter in the universe, and it must be righted by punishment: an eye for an eye and a tooth for a tooth remains with us all, though we may be unaware of it.

This assaultive idea is particularly relevant to a discussion of parent-child relationship. The idea of the turning of an adult to a child as uncontingent on the child's behavior is difficult and elusive for us. It seems more promising somehow to offer the child a reward for compliance with the adult's wishes. Actually, however, such manipulative techniques are quite impotent in accomplishing anything more than superficial—and usually short-lived—compliance. Children can see through the thin veneer of these techniques and are often quite scornful of them. A child in the clinic school, for example, in response to the effort of a Social Worker to lure him into compliance through some tempting bait, said, matter-of-factly, "It won't work."

Such a manipulative attitude, Barth would say, derives from the religious position of attempting to manipulate God and finds its secondary expression in the attempt to manipulate people. It is another manifestation of the attitude, mentioned above, that places in an ultimate position reliance on the wielding of one's own power, i.e., idolatry.

The distinction between a manipulative stance toward children and a stance of prevenient and uncontingent moving toward a child is particularly interesting to me because of the contrast I have personally observed in the way these two positions have affected children of my acquaintance. I think especially of children like William, who try the patience of all adults because they have such difficulty controlling their behavior. At the clinic school in the institution where William was a patient, there are gathered some forty children who are hospitalized, not because they are mentally incapable, but because they cannot control their actions; they are constantly susceptible to being overrun by their own destructive impulses. Under certain circumstances the scene at the hospital can suddenly take on the appearance of a battlefield; aggression is unleashed in all directions, each attack provoking counterattack; they hit and curse and tear at each other until some adult police action intervenes to gain tenuous control—until the next explosion.

The adults responsible for these children are of course concerned to find some way to prevent this kind of behavior from recurring, and the way that seems logical and promising to many is some plan to manipulate the children's compliance through control of gratification. There is, in fact, a popular school of psychology that is based on such a plan, that is, to attempt to bring about effective change in behavior through the manipulation of rewards based on certain performance.

It is of course true that children will go to great lengths to gain the rewards, especially children who, for whatever reason, have been short on supplies of all kinds; it is this fact that contributes to the error in perception, i.e., the view that these techniques, after all, "work." However, such manipulation "works" in a very circumscribed way, namely a compliance toward authority to the degree necessary to gain the rewards. It also works, in a rather effective way, to communicate a philosophy of materialistic gain through conformity.

It is interesting to ponder how symbols and relationship are utilized by this method: the symbols of nourishment are no longer representative of the good breast, generous and free, but are converted into implements of power. The relationship uses the position of power to control—however disguised the tyranny—rather than to sustain and support the child's emerging being. The contrast in an attitude of forcing compliance and one of sustenance will be clearer as we proceed; at this point, it is enough to mention that manipulation is powerless to evoke any deep motivational change.

What does evoke genuine change of motivation and behavior in these impulse-ridden children is a mode of relating to them that has this "can't earn" quality. It is an attitude of a prevenient, uncontingent offering of the ego of the caring adult in a freely given alliance with the ego of the child against the destructive impulse, *which is then revealed to the child also as alien and undesirable*. This stance of offering to lend aid to the child's person against a common enemy can be expressed quite simply to a child trapped in his own aggression: "You seem to be having trouble with your hands this morning—try holding on to me." "I have to stop you," (firmly, but not angrily restraining the child), "that hitting is not good for you." "If your feet are giving you trouble, sit on them." "That stick is no help to you—give it to me." "You are very angry and need some help. I will hold you right here until you can get your hands under control."

While such phrases as these are not magical in themselves, they derive from an attitude of being *with*, not *against*, the child, and this attitude has an effect not unlike what Barth refers to as the difference in a response of gratitude as opposed to "a tribute to tyranny" (1957, p. 219). Obedience obtained from a child as a tribute to the tyranny of an adult, however disguised as reward for good behavior, is quite different from the obedience that is the spontaneous offering of gratitude for the free, uncontingent gift of the person of the adult in alliance against the alien force. It is also striking that a child recognizes the destructive force as alien to himself only in the light of such a relationship, a fact that brings us back to Barth's point that the true situation of human beings and their idols is revealed only in God's grace happening to them.

It was the power of perception gained through a new kind of relationship that enabled William, for example, to see that his wild animals were not going to be needed anymore. He had begun to move from a position of the "I must," to a position of "I may and I can" (Käsemann, 1965). A part of that new position was the beginning of recognition of an alien part of himself that was "in the way," to use his own words.

Grace is unhindered by unworthiness or opposition. Again, it is these children who are hospitalized because they are overrun with destructive urges who illustrate what I think Barth means by this characteristic of grace. I have observed that a mode of relating to the children that is informed by the nature of grace is distinguishable by a greater invulnerability to the rage and aggression of the child. The adult, without doubt, can be vulnerable and provoked into aggression also. But when given an attitude of grace, the attitude itself is not affected by unworthiness or opposition. When the grace is present, its power over enmity against it reveals itself. The level of aggression has no effect on it, while the grace distinctly has an effect on the level of aggression. This fact reveals to us where the real power lies.

For example, let us consider the child who was mentioned above in connection with moving from a position of "ruthlessness to ruth," of unconcern to concern. As powerful as his destructive aggression was, and as angry as it could make me feel when he turned it against me, the aggression never weakened the power that was pitted against it, namely the power of the "cannot earn" gift. It was the persistence of the offering of the free gift, in alliance with a part of him that had begun to recognize the alien quality of his destructive urges, that communicated the message that there was something bigger and more powerful than his own bad feelings. Each time he discovered—in joyous relief—that

A Theological Perspective

this bigger reality survived his aggression, he learned to lean more heavily on the good feelings instead of the bad feelings inside himself.

Grace precedes law, not vice-versa. The children speak to us again in a way that helps to make clear what Barth is saying.

Rules and regulations, or the order of law, have little meaning for youngsters like William—except as a source of fear of punishment or loss of reward—until they have experienced a relationship characterized by acceptance and respect. It is as though there is no awareness of the possibility of another kind of behavior, no goal at all toward which to move, no standard from which they can judge as inadequate the behavior in which they are trapped. The measurement of their own actions by another standard is available to them only after an experience of the kind of relationship that can be described as grace-full. It is the gift without strings *first* that creates the capacity for the perception of new possibilities. Grace, according to Barth, *creates a capacity that is not already there.* It is by means of the new capacity of discernment that the undesirability of the destructive impulse becomes revealed to the child and the interest in mastering it emerges.

Clinically speaking, one could say that the "observing ego," the ability to be aware of one's own actions in reference to some inwardly perceived standard, is achieved in the personality on the basis of a new object relation. Love and trust have to be learned from someone who is able to give first. This statement reminds us again of Klein's emphasis on the good breast as fundamental in personality formation, especially in the ability to achieve the depressive position, with its corollary of the ability to shoulder one's own ambivalence. To attempt to make children "responsible" along the line of law, namely that arrangement whereby infringement of rules equals punishment, obedience equals rewards, prior to extending acceptance, is to begin at the wrong place. One begins with the free gift of acceptance. It is the response of gratitude, not forced compliance, that engenders true obedience.

Grace is inherently powerful and overcomes enmity against it without violating the self-determination of those in the grip of the enmity. The quality of grace that Barth refers to here is particularly important for us in thinking about the parent-child relationship because it offers a means to grasp the real issue involved in the matter of discipline. A firm allegiance to the idea of discipline versus permissiveness as the issue lends itself easily to the erroneous notion common in parents and educators that their responsibility is to force the compliance of children to their own will. In its crudest form, this attitude is expressed as the necessity to "break the will" of a child.

As mentioned above, Sullivan quite effectively laid this misconception to rest with his clear discernment and sharp wit (1953, p. 173). The issue is not one of discipline versus permissiveness; it is, rather, whether the relationship with the child is wired so that the will of the child is forced to comply with the will of the adult, either by overt tyranny or by covert control, or whether the respect for the child's own being is maintained in a relationship informed by the nature of grace.[1]

A relationship informed by the nature of grace would mean that the parent takes up the position toward the child in a way analogous to the way God loves us into loving without compelling or forcing our self-determination. The informed parent, or teacher, understands that the true power does not lie in the violation of the child's own being by open or hidden tyranny. A new order has been revealed in grace that has transcended the kind of power represented by tyranny[2] and has disclosed the impotence inherent in *quid-pro-quo*, this-for-that, kind of thinking.

William, who had such trouble with "hitting people in the face," manifests the relative power of an attitude informed by grace and one of forced compliance. For most of his few years, William had been subjected to attempts to control him by various methods, generally based on "what he deserved." What he deserved was mostly punishment, which led to more anger, which led to more punishment. The impotence of that line of power is thus revealed. The power that reached him, that enabled him to subdue the wild animals, was the power of a relationship in which uncontingent, prevenient acceptance came first, allying itself with him and not against him.

Grace, in my view, is the most precise and useful concept by which we can understand the new kind of power by which he was able to come forth and realize aspects of his true self which previously had

---

[1] Compare with Winnicott's view that "compliance is a sick basis for life:" "Compliance carries with it a sense of futility for the individual and is associated with the idea that nothing matters and that life is not worth living" (1971, p. 65).

[2] For a discussion of this subject as it informs the clinical treatment of a child overrun by malign destructive urges, see Martyn, "A Child and Adam: A Parable of the Two Ages."

A Theological Perspective

been hidden, for example, his ability to learn. Something called forth life in him, and that something was grace. He had come into contact with the reality of that force through participation in it via the symbol—that is, the dough and the cake, and he manifested its reality for him also through a symbol, the new street.

Holiness

As grace reveals one aspect of God's love, so the dialectic statement of God's holiness refers, says Barth, to one aspect of his freedom. The concept of holiness affirms that God does not surrender Himself to the object of his graciousness.

> He neither compromises with his resistance, nor ignores it, still less calls it good. But as the gracious God He affirms Himself over against the one to whom He is gracious by opposing and breaking down his resistance, and in some way causing His own good will to exert its effect upon him. Therefore the one to whom He is gracious comes to experience God's opposition to him (1957, p. 361).

> For whom the Lord loveth He correcteth; even as a father the son in whom he delighteth (Proverbs 3:12) (p. 361).

Barth is referring here to a *tension* thus established between God and his creatures, and this tension can be seen to have a derivative in the parent-child relationship. The good will of the parent figure toward a child caught in his own destructive impulses does not result in the adult's giving over in weakness to the will and behavior of the child. The aggressive behavior that is destructive is actively opposed; the child is not abandoned to it nor is it sanctioned.

As indicated above, the issue is not permissiveness. God does not join us in our rebellion but actively opposes it; similarly, the parent who is informed by God's prior way stands in loving and firm opposition to hurtful behavior on the part of the child. Thus there is a tension that is felt in the relationship that is not dissolved by the abdication of the parent. But the opposition manifested toward the destructive behavior is not divisible from or contradictory to the gracious love; the tension-opposite is the other side of the love, just as:

> The holiness of God consists in the unity of His judgment with his grace. God is holy because His grace judges and His judgment is gracious (1957, p. 363).

What we learn from this tension in God's grace with his holiness, in terms of parents and children, can be illustrated by the situation with the child mentioned in connection with "ruthlessness and ruth," or, in fact, any of these hospitalized children suffering from lack of inner control. Had I abandoned this child to his own destructive urges, out of some misguided notion of permissiveness that ignored a "strong opposition to the enemy," the grace would have been rendered inoperative. He would have been turned over to his own powerlessness against his enemy. Therefore the tension inherent in the reality of grace with a stance of strength against its opposition is essential to its nature and is an important aspect of its derivative in the parent-child relationship.

The Mercy and Righteousness of God

Mercy

In exploring further the meaning of the statement that God is the One who Loves in Freedom, Barth distinguishes the quality of mercy as an aspect of God's love, in dialectic with the quality of righteousness, as an expression of his freedom. As God's grace refers to his turning on his own initiative toward humankind, his mercy implies his participation in and determination speedily to relieve the distress of the creature:

> It lies, therefore, in His will, springing from the depths of His nature and characterising it, to take the initiative Himself for the removal of this distress. For the fact that God participates in it by sympathy implies that He is really present in its midst, and this means again that he wills that it should not be, that He wills therefore to remove it (1957, p. 369).

Barth makes clear here that what is involved is not merely a sentiment but is power and deed. God addresses himself in power and active concern to the distress, suffering, misery, folly, bondage, and torment, which are the manifestations of our resistance to grace and the

A Theological Perspective

reliance on our own arrogant idolatry (p. 371). God addresses this situation by taking the suffering upon Himself, in the very gift of his son:

> Because our sin and guilt are now in the heart of God, they are no longer exclusively ours. Because He bears them, the suffering and punishment from them are lifted from us, and our own suffering can be only a reminiscence of His (p. 374).

We can—again derivatively and secondarily—thus understand the nature of the mercy of human beings to other human beings, and a parent's mercy to a child, as the gift of being enabled effectually to participate in the misery of another.

Thinking God's thoughts after him, it is not only relevant, but central to address ourselves to the suffering of such small ones as William, and those hundreds like him, who are the present-day representatives of the poor, the weak, the defenseless whom God addressed in Israel. Effectual compassion for these children, active participation in their distress with intention speedily to relieve it is mediated mercy. Of course the distress of these children is a miniature of a wider social distress, which calls us to this same attitude of "active participation in their distress with intention speedily to relieve it."

It does not appear natural to human beings to move toward this suffering; it appears rather that it is more natural to turn away from it, to push it out of sight, reject those who manifest it, and to punish and incarcerate its representatives. To those informed by the ways of God's loving, the call is, rather, to participate in the suffering, to take our place in the shadow of the crucifixion, where the ultimate meaning of suffering and death have been borne (p. 395):

> And we cannot live in the neighbourhood of Golgotha without being affected by the shadow of divine judgment, without allowing this shadow to fall on us. In this shadow Israel suffered. In this shadow the Church suffers....That suffering should be learned in this shadow is in I Peter the problem of faith for every Christian community and individual Christian. "Nay, in all these things we are more than conquerors through him that loved us" (Rom. 8:37). The shadow would not fall if the cross of Christ did not stand in the light of His resurrection. We would not have to suffer if it were not that we are "begotten again unto a lively hope by the resurrection of Jesus Christ from the dead" (I Pet. 1:3) (p. 406).

Righteousness

The righteousness of God refers to the way in which God, in his covenant relationship with human beings, remains true to his own being. The issue here is what befits and is worthy of him (p. 386). Barth's emphasis is that God maintains his own worthiness and that his righteousness includes enabling the creature to maintain what befits and is worthy of the creature. God as the maker of his covenant with human beings issues a summons:

> [A summons] with which He lifts us out of all the being and doing in which we try to follow our own ideas of justice, i.e., what befits and is worthy of us. Faith in God's righteousness means necessarily and essentially a choice and decision in favour of His righteousness as opposed to our own; in other words, the choice and decision by which instead of our own righteousness we accept as our own the righteousness of God, or according to the shorter New Testament definition, of Christ (1957, p. 386).

In thinking of William, and all those others who, like him, had no effective parent, what strikes me as relevant here is the emphasis that God's righteousness, from Israel's first encounter with it, had the nature of right in favor of the threatened innocent, the oppressed poor, widows, orphans, and aliens" (p. 386):

> For this reason, in the relations and events in the life of His people, God always takes His stand unconditionally and passionately on this side and on this side alone: against the lofty and on behalf of the lowly; against those who already enjoy right and privilege and on behalf of those who are denied and deprived of it....It does in fact have this character and we cannot hear it and believe it without feeling a sense of responsibility in the direction indicated (p. 386).

Thus the indissoluble connection between God's mercy, his compassionate involvement in human misery, and his righteousness is revealed:

> ...The truth emerges that God's righteousness does not really stand alongside His mercy, but that as revealed in its necessary connexion, according to scripture, with the plight of the poor and wretched, it is itself God's mercy (p. 387).

A major implication of these words for the person attempting to address troubled children who cannot help themselves is that the

A Theological Perspective

helper is in fact standing on common ground with them. It is understood that one's own relationship to God's righteousness consists only in embracing the faith of "those who are poor and wretched before God." "When we encounter divine righteousness we are all like the people of Israel, menaced and altogether lost according to their own strength. We are all widows and orphans who cannot procure right for themselves" (p. 387). Why, asks Barth, are we summoned to espouse the cause of the poor? The human being is so summoned

> because in them it is manifested to him what he himself is in the sight of God; because the living, gracious, merciful action of God towards him consists in the fact that God Himself in His own righteousness procures right for him, the poor and wretched; because he and all men stand in the presence of God, as those for whom right can be procured only by God Himself....As surely as he himself lives by the grace of God he cannot evade this claim (p. 387).

Thus comes the insight that, for those who address themselves to children in need, the meaning of mercy and righteousness, which is derivative from God's mercy and righteousness, is the contiguity of their own state of poverty before God as recipients of mercy with the state of the children. There is, therefore, precluded the stance of a superior, who is able to dispense rightness and security to those whom he feels to be in an inferior position.

The Patience and Wisdom of God

Patience

Patience exists where space and time are given with a definite intention, where freedom is allowed in expectation of a response (1957, p. 408).

Again Barth moves from God's self-disclosure to the human scene. God has allowed space and time for the existence of his creatures; he has conceded to the existence and reality of another, alongside his own. As Barth illustrates at length from such scriptural examples as the pledge of God to sustain the life of Cain and the story of Noah, God does not act in such a way as to violate the space and time of the other, rather,

> We define God's patience as His will, deep-rooted in His essence and constituting His divine being and action, to allow to another—for the sake of His own grace and mercy and in the affirmation of His holiness and justice—space and time for the development of its own existence, thus conceding to this existence a reality side by side with His own, and fulfilling His will towards this other in such a way that He does not suspend and destroy it as this other but accompanies and sustains it and allows it to develop in freedom (p. 409f).

God does not blot out the reality of the other's being.

> [God] deals with His creature in such a way as to share his wretchedness. This is the meaning of His mercy. In this way it is more powerful than if it had to kill and slay in order to arrive at its goal. It is so powerful that it can wait, allowing us to continue (p. 411).

The creaturely forms of this way of God's loving reflect those same qualities. It is precisely this quality of "sustaining and accompanying" the other, allowing the other to develop in freedom (i.e., in its being true to its own self), which characterizes the wise parent, the true teacher, and the authentic therapist.

Winnicott, whose writing has been so germane to my investigation, seems in his work to breathe this quality of respect for the personhood of the other, in which the therapist can be "patient" and can sustain the other's being—however fragmented it may be—until the patient himself begins to move, to grow, and change:

> If only we can wait, the patient arrives at understanding creatively and with immense joy, and I now enjoy this joy more than I used to enjoy the sense of having been clever....The principle is that it is the patient and only the patient who has the answers. We may or may not enable him or her to encompass what is known or become aware of it with acceptance (Winnicott, 1971, p. 87).

There is a profound difference in the attitude of the parental figure here from any point of view that proceeds from the assumption that one party possesses the desirable traits toward which he can guide the other through a series of manipulations. This difference, in my perception, derives from the quality of patience as it has been made known to us in God's self-disclosure. This paradigm of allowance and respect for the other's space and time potentially informs not only the parent-child relationship, but all other human relationships in which genuine mutuality is at issue, including that of male-female, both individually and collectively. This attitude precludes the assaultive stance of any party toward another, requiring that the other concede to the position of power or superiority, whether political, ideological, or moral. To be informed by this patience of God is to be able to sustain and accompany the other without forcing the hand according to one's own judgment, without violating the space and time of this other being.

Wisdom

God's wisdom refers to the fact that God knows what he is doing. There is no higher abstraction by which God's intelligence and rationality can be judged; rather is it that he is steadfast, consistent, not impulsive or irrational. The whys and wherefores, the therefores and the reasons rest in God alone. This quality stands in dialectic to his patience, as a form of his freedom to a form of his love. Because he is wise, he can allow space and existence to another without uncertainty or danger. Wisdom is God's own self-explanation, which is subject to no higher appeal.

The creature side of wisdom, says Barth, is in heeding and accepting God's wisdom:

> Divine wisdom is obviously the meaning and ground of creation and therefore of the sphere in which man can live. The whole art of living and understanding life consists in heeding and accepting divine wisdom and in this way becoming wise (1957, p. 430).

Barth makes clear in the same passage from which this excerpt is taken that human wisdom is quite different from abstract reasoning or from the "ability to extract silver and gold and iron and brass from the bowels of the earth." It consists in recognizing "that in the world we are given space and ground to learn how to live in the presence of this holy and righteous One and in covenant with Him a life which is in keeping with His being revealed in the establishment and execution of this covenant, to the end that we might thus live the only possible life" (p. 430). In briefer and more familiar terms, "Behold, the fear of the Lord, that is wisdom; and to depart from evil is understanding" (Job 28:28) (p. 431). While human wisdom means the art of living, of making use of life "which is in harmony with its creation and preservation by God and therefore rich and meaningful, rich in promise and redemptive" (p. 433), it must be noted that:

> Human wisdom of this kind is not a possibility which man can intrinsically realise. It is a gift of God which has to be sought. It springs from a special divine grace and favour (p. 433).

And, even more succinctly:

> In short, it cannot be possessed by man as in the last analysis all other treasures cannot be possessed by him (p. 431).

Thus, the dialectical statement concerning God's patience and wisdom, namely that God can give human beings space and time and that God knows what he is doing, informs the specific human situation that we are considering—the parent-child relationship in its widest meaning—in this way: we can allow children space and time, without violating them, because God knows what he is doing, and we endeavor to recognize that wisdom and to align our thoughts and acts accordingly.

These attempts to look at the relevance of the ways of God to the ways of human beings in a specific context point to a common theme, that is, that for all of us, these qualities of relationship are not primary; they are mediated. Grace and holiness, mercy and righteousness, patience and wisdom are dependent on a higher source than humankind. There is something of *receivership* as the condition under which we can manifest any of them. We can turn in freely given, undeserved compassion only secondarily to having first been the recipient. "Because he first loved us" is the profound basis of all human graciousness.

Similarly, as we have seen, the very essence of "mercy and righteousness" for the human being is the stance of *emptyhandedness*, on common ground with all God's children, as those for whom right can be procured only by God Himself. The patience "to allow space and time to the other" comes out of faith in God's wisdom, that he knows what he is doing, and therefore we can rest in that sure confidence in facilitating in others the freedom to be who one is. The truth—that the human stance is emptyhandedness before God and the sure

A Theological Perspective

confidence in his ways—must be part of the meaning that we "must become as little children." Thus it emerges that the mediated, derivative quality of human ways is itself central to our understanding of them.

Barth never leaves us in doubt that the medium through which God's ways are made known to us is the humanity of Jesus Christ, as shown in the scriptures. Jesus Christ is the embodiment of God's prior turning toward human beings, "the complete, all-embracing divine action for man" (1957, p. 364).

> The revelation of this name as the epitome of the expectation of Israel and the recollection of the Church is also in Holy Scripture the epitome of the reality of God's mercy. We cannot get behind this name to learn why God is merciful. But we can infer from this name with unshakable certainty that He is (p. 373).

Further,

> In the mystery of God called Christ "are hid all the treasures of wisdom and knowledge" and...Jesus Christ is the meaning of God's patience...p. 432).

For me, the most powerful witness Barth makes in regard to Jesus Christ is that

> He accepted God's grace in our place and therefore rendered to God the obedience which we continually refuse (p. 152).

It is the extremity of our enmity against grace, the refusal of forgiveness itself that Jesus Christ overcame. He

> has not only borne man's enmity against God's grace, revealing it in all its depth. He has borne the far greater burden, the righteous wrath of God against those who are enemies of His grace, the wrath which must fall on us. For it is we who are enemies of the grace of God. *It is we who do that which by its very nature cannot be forgiven, because it is the despising of forgiveness itself* (p. 152).[Italics mine.]

At the point of taking up the framework of Karl Barth as a way of looking at qualities of relationship, that is, as perceiving them as derivative from and secondary to God's ways of loving us first, I am aware that I have crossed a line, a divide, in intellectual disciplines, and

I am aware also that I have taken a stance that involves an attitude of faith as well as an attitude of investigation. In any attempt to understand human journeys from one point to another, one always arrives at ultimate questions, and, in fact, one always begins and ends an intellectual endeavor with an implicit, if not an explicit, premise of faith in what one believes to be ultimate.[3]

It is my view that, while the children's journeys as they stand and the clinical investigation in theoretical terms have been enlightening per se, it is Barth's inversion of the telescope—his reversal of our ordinary order of regarding things human and things ultimate—that has offered the more complete view of the qualities of relationship that make possible any human metamorphosis. In the next and final chapter, I will come to some conclusions as to what I believe I have discovered in the course of this investigation.

---

[3] The "prejudice against prejudice," as a questionable heritage from the Enlightenment, has been illumined by Hans-Georg Gadamer (1972, p. 239f.).

Chapter IX

CONCLUSION

Barth's paradigm offers us a new line of vision by which to survey the children's journeys. It also offers a way of looking at the questions raised at the end of Chapter I as to how the children's use of symbol and the contextual relationship were related to the personality changes. The clue to the new means of perception is the *direction of the line of movement by which the forces of change are activated.*

Human growth is generally understood to proceed in a line of movement originating in the human subject. In looking back to the children's journeys, I would certainly affirm that forces for growth and maturation are very much in evidence. I believe, however, that the activating of these forces is dependent on a prior line of movement, that is, God's own action in moving toward us.

Behold, I do a new thing

says the prophet, Isaiah, and the subject of the verb is not a human being, but God. I believe that it is God's new deed that is the dynamism by which we understand most profoundly the human notion of "sublimation." The "sublime" is actually not a what, toward which we move, but, more fundamentally, a Who, who moves toward us.

How does this shift in perspective affect our understanding of Amy, John, and William and their growing in the course of their symbolic play?

Barth asserted that God makes himself known in power and deed, in act, in happening, as we learned in the last chapter. We also made note there that "Grace is inherently powerful." Powerful to do what?

There is one New Testament author who spoke most directly to this question, and that author was Paul, the apostle. *Grace* is one of the key words by which Paul points to God's powerful invasion of the human sphere, the sphere where he sees human beings to be held in bondage, or, to use the more radical word, slavery. The power holding human beings in bondage, in servitude, Paul refers to as *Sin*. *Sin*, like grace, is also a summary word; it points to the power that enslaves human beings and holds them in its grip. It is an entity clearly to be distinguished from its popular definition of misdeeds, or various unethical actions (Romans 6:16; 7:7-14). A brief statement that clarifies the nature of this entity is found in Romans 5:20:

> As sin established its reign by way of death, so God's grace might establish its reign in righteousness.

The words here are difficult but pregnant with meaning for the task at hand. Let us take two of the key concepts in the approach of Paul, that of bondage, and that of *Sin*. The theologian Paul Tillich makes their usefulness in understanding the children immediately accessible: he speaks of healing as deliverance from *bondage*.

> We consider the neurotic or psychotic person who cannot face life as sick. But if we describe his disease, we find that *he is under the power of compulsions from which he cannot extricate himself* (Tillich, 1963, p. 93). [Italics mine.]

He illumines with equal simplicity the nature of Sin, which he describes as *separation*.

> To be in the state of sin is to be in the state of separation. And separation is threefold: there is separation among individual lives, separation of a man from himself, and separation of all men from the Ground of Being (1948, p. 154f.).

Conclusion

It is the children who can best explicate for us the meaning of these two concepts. All three were suffering from bondage, that is, from the power of compulsions from which they could not extricate themselves. All three were suffering, in addition, from separation: separation from others, from themselves, and from the Ground of Being, to use Tillich's terms.

Amy, for example, was separated from much of her own vitality; she had to isolate much of her impulse life in a doghouse, distant from her own dwelling. She had a compulsion to "wear a mask," to "keep getting up and running around," to use the language of her dreams, to "star" in the eyes of all adults. Her nervous tics were a clue that "her animals were in captivity," as she stated the situation of her repression. There were aspects of her own being from which she was estranged, and she expressed her separation from other people by withdrawing into books.

John was separated from his own power. The opening bars of his overture to play were: "He's always going forward, but his car is always left behind." John was also in bondage, caught in compulsion; he was compelled always to lose. He was in bondage to the fear of being "too fast and too good," and he was separated from his own supplies of "oxygen" and "gas." Without these vital supplies, his hero was in danger of "drowning," and his world was "like a graveyard,... where it was necessary for him to scratch himself out a little room." This picture of the death-like grip of alien forces is very close to the thought of Paul above, "As sin established its reign by way of death."

William was suffering under the compulsion to "hit people in the face," and his servitude to his own rage was separating him from other people. The tyranny of his own aggression had him firmly in its grip, and he was driven to project his negative feelings to the outside and attack them "out there." William was also separated from his own powers of learning and creating; cut off even from his own tears, from any capacity to feel empathically with others; separated from the nourishment, internally and externally, from the good breast that he had been denied.

Thus we see that Amy, John, and William were in a state of bondage, in Paul's meaning of the word, and in a state of separation from others and from aspects of their own being.

From the line of vision provided by Barth's paradigm, and drawing on the insights provided by Paul, what now can be said about relationship and symbol and change?

To be quite certain of our direction, let us return to the lens through which we are trying now to see. What, according to Paul, invades this sphere of bondage and liberates its hostages? Or rather, in Paul *Who* invades this territory of bondage and sets the hostages free? God, says Paul, invades this realm of slavery, not by principles or new teachings, but by a *person*, Jesus Christ.

> We cannot get behind this name to learn why God is merciful. But we can infer from this name with unshakable certainty that He is (Barth, 1957, p. 373).

From the first records of God's dealings with Israel, we know that we are never dealing with What, but always with Whom.

> Hast thou not known, hast thou not heard
> that firm remains on high
> The everlasting throne of Him
> who form'd the earth and sky? (Isaiah 40:2)

and

> All thine iniquities who doth
> most graciously forgive;
> Who thy diseases all and pains
> doth heal and thee relieve.
> Who doth redeem thy life, that thou
> to death may'st not go down;
> Who thee with loving-kindness doth
> and tender mercies crown; (Psalm 103, Scottish Psalter).

Israel repeatedly found that it was an intensely personal covenant with Jahweh with which they were bound, that the whole meaning of their existence was that they lived "in the fear of the Lord," that is to say, that they existed in the hands of Another. This acknowledgement that life consists of existence within the circle of relationship, of "being in the hands of Another," is surely the fundamental truth by which we understand all the kinds of relationship addressed in these pages: the relationship of children and parents, in the widest sense, as well as the

Conclusion

transference relationship in psychotherapy. Relationship, as pointed to by Barth, is in the very nature of the Godhead—as attested by the doctrine of the Trinity—, and it is in keeping with God's own being that he seeks to regrasp his creatures by invading their sphere of bondage through a person, his own Son. His way is to draw human beings into a community characterized by participation in his Son, Jesus Christ. It is through him that "he makes alive the dead and calls into being the things that are not" (Romans 4:17).

Human beings drawn into participation within a circle of another—this is the paradigm. But how? How are we drawn into the circle of this other?

From the beginnings of the Church, believers have participated in the person of Jesus Christ through the sacraments, or—for communions who say it differently—"the means of grace." What are the sacraments or the means of grace? They are those special ways by which the presence of the resurrected Lord is made known to us, ways in which we are given to experience this reality, to register it, to appropriate it.

Let us take the Eucharistic meal, or the Lord's Supper, as it is otherwise termed. Whatever the differences in practice or interpretation of this memorial meal, there is one irreducible common feature in its observance—the elements of bread and wine, and these elements *stand for something*.

> During supper he took bread, and having said the blessing he broke it and gave it to them, with the words "Take this; this is my body." Then he took a cup....And he said, `This is my blood, the blood of the covenant, shed for many....(Mark 14:23-24).

The presence of the risen Lord is thus conveyed to us through something that stands for him, through a *symbol* of his presence. Cyril Richardson, mentioned previously in a discussion of Christian symbolism (1955) makes two statements that are helpful in understanding this point. Reviewing:

> [Symbols] are our way of becoming aware, of registering meanings. Indeed, most of reality is not accessible to us without symbols; for it is by symbols that we come into contact with it. What the symbol does is to give reality meaning so that we can participate in it (p. 2).

> The symbol forms our contact with different aspects of reality, because it makes of them an intelligible whole. It brings together a society, knitting it into a cohesive group. And, finally, the symbol comprehends a great number of meanings and relationships, bringing them together into a single unit so that their intimate connection with each other may not be lost (p. 10).

In discussing the Eucharistic meal, he says:

> There is no symbolism more gripping than that of eating and drinking. It expresses in the deepest way the idea of participation. One becomes what one eats, and food is the very source of one's existence. It is for these reasons that feasting has always played a large role in cult practices. It is the bond which unites a fellowship with the closest ties; and the sacrificial imagery implied in the slaying of animals finds its consummation in the banquet that follows....(p. 15).

In summing up the way in which Eucharistic symbolism brought together for the early church the central themes of the Christian faith, he states:

> This recalling was more realistically conceived than in most current Protestantism. An image, a symbol, or a dramatic representation was more than a sign or token. It implied that the image or "type" shared in the reality to which it pointed and which it conveyed. What we have already said about the dynamic power of symbols applies with peculiar force to the sacraments. They are the way by which the heavenly reality is made accessible. They participate in it, making it intelligible and bringing it within our reach (p. 18).

Thus Richardson has affirmed the same emphasis made by Paul Tillich, who also maintained that the symbol does more than "point to" a reality, it also participates in the power of what is represented (Tillich, 1955).

Here it seems that we have the model for understanding how the children's use of symbol and the relationship in which it occurred were connected. The model shows us an invasion of a sphere of bondage, in Paul's terms, where human beings are caught in compulsions from which they cannot extricate themselves and in separation from each other and themselves. The invader is a Person, into whose circle a community is drawn, and into whose sphere of power they are brought in. Participation in this sphere of relationship and its power has always involved, even in the diversity of confessions, the incorporation through symbolic elements of the presence of the Lord. What can we derive from this paradigm, secondarily?

I have asserted in the course of this essay that my view of the way the children used the symbolic play is that through it they "ate"—incorporated—a new object relationship. The child who showed me periodically how large and strong his arm muscle had grown "because of the tea," and William, who by way of the dough and the cake was able to discover possibilities in himself—a "new street" that eliminated his need for wild animals—found in these symbolic elements a means of appropriating a human presence. Through images of nourishment, which are in their very nature *participatory*, as Richardson showed us, they were able to incorporate the vital force present in this other person, and, through their symbolic play, they gave expression to their own enlarged boundaries, their discoveries of parts of themselves previously undiscovered or split off by repression. They were able to mobilize their own vital force into new creations through its being aroused in the relationship.

The children's creations, as we have seen, spoke their own messages more clearly than any explication of them. Of course we can point to certain things each symbol may have represented: Freud's insight reveals the instinctual underlayers; Jung's, the transformation by analogue of libido from the unconscious to the conscious sphere so that the ego has new access to it; Klein's emphasis on the tie to the object world and all reality. The symbols apparently served as bridges in the overcoming of the bondage and separation that have been the focus of this conclusion—bridges to other people, and to their own undiscovered and unrealized parts.[1] However, it would be a disservice to reduce the communications of the children to any of these explanations. Each of the children's images was a coalescence of many meanings into the

---

[1] Winnicott illustrates this *connecting* use of the symbol and points out its simultaneous function as an image of *separateness* in his observations of a child's use of string:

> Sometimes he would make a gesture which was as if he 'plugged in' with the end of the string like an electric flex to his mother's thigh. One had to observe that...he was using the string as a symbol of union with his mother. It was clear that the string was simultaneously a symbol of separateness and of union through communication (1971, p. 43).

most concise and complete statement possible for the expression of ideas and feelings which lay "beyond the net of language and logic," as a poet put it. These creations were signs of new being that speak for themselves.

Amy, for example, kept sounding the theme that her old house was "too small and too crowded," and her mind's eye began to create larger and nobler living spaces. The spiraling snail; the metamorphosis of animals in captivity into the dancing worm; the series of transformations of the tightly containing "big box" into the open cage and finally into the bird-bath, with its life-giving possibilities of water and air—these speak a message of more abundant life.

As a last creation before Amy left the playroom with its special shelter, she made a boat from card-board and paper, no doubt as an expression of her launching out—on her own—into new waters. She pondered aloud what her boat might need. First she provided it with paddles, suggesting a means of directing it where she wanted it to go. She then added sails, so that her boat could get power from the wind; a cover of waxed paper for the hulk, as means for protection; ropes, by which she could control the sails, i.e., the power. "It needs something else," she said. Her eye fell on a life-saver, a cardboard circle which she had made earlier to supply a lovely pool-house that had been her final rendition of finer dwellings. When she had made the life-saver, she had remarked that "the people in the house like to keep the life-saver where they can see it. You see, it saved someone a long time ago." In equipping her boat for launching, she suddenly decided that this life-saver should go along. This paper circle thus provided a bridge between the encircling relationship it represented and the new life she was sailing into, symbolized by her boat.

There is one aspect of the children's use of these dramatic representations that needs final emphasis, that is, the paradox that it was precisely through their rendering of images of their *wounds* that gave rise to their claiming aspects of their being from which they had been estranged. This fact has been mentioned briefly in regard to Amy's use of her isolated doghouse, which in time enabled her to overcome her separation from her vitality. Similarly, John's first theme in his play had given rise to a symphonic poem around the tiny flaw in the arm of the toy soldier. It was this sense of being wounded, damaged, that inspired the months of work in the course of which he overcame the separation from his own power. William also found it to be the wild animals—his own destructive urges—that gave him the clue to wider avenues.

The children here bring to mind Heine's picture of God in the Creation, which Freud referred to in his paper on Narcissism: God is imagined as saying, "Illness was no doubt the final cause of the whole urge to create. By creating, I could recover; by creating, I became healthy" [Erschaffend wurde ich gesund] (Freud, 1914, p. 85).

There is a profound theme sounded here, which must underlie also the words of the Psalm,

> That stone is made head cornerstone,
> which builders did despise:
> This is the doing of the Lord,
> And wondrous in our eyes.

There are theological depths in these words to which the present essay can only point. Is this a way of saying that the invasion of the sphere of bondage takes captive the very representatives of death and uses them for life? And is there some reality implied here that would shed light both on Freud's idea of the fusion of instincts and Jung's insistence that there is a place for Evil in the Godhead? Do these speculations about Eros and Thanatos, and about tension between opposites, bear witness unawares to the theology of the Cross? These questions point beyond themselves to others, to a mystery that lies beyond this inquiry.

The children's journeys provided the impetus for the pilgrimage this essay has recorded, and thus Amy, John, and William enlarged my own boundaries. They contribute their part also to the larger picture to which we heard Barth refer, that we all stand before God as little children, as recipients of his mercy and grace. The good breast, by which we must all be nourished, has this ultimate source:

See the streams of living water, flowing from Eternal Love
Well supply their sons and daughters, and all fear of want remove.
Who can faint, while such a river, ever flows their thirst to assuage
Grace, which like the Lord, the giver, never fails from age to age.

REFERENCES

Aite, P. (1978). Ego and Image. Some Observations on the Theme of "Sand Play." *The Journal of Analytical Psychology, 23* (4), 332-338.

Bachelard, G. (1958). *The Poetics of Space.* New York: Orion Press, 1964.

Balint, M. (1952). On Love and Hate. *International Journal of Psycho-Analysis, 33,* 355-362.

Barrett, C. K. (1962). *From First Adam to Last.* London: Adam and Charles Black.

Barth, K. (1957). *Church Dogmatics* (Vol. II/1). Edinburgh: T & T Clark.

Barth, K. (1961). *Church Dogmatics.* (Vol. III/4). Edinburgh: T & T Clark.

Benedek, T. (1938). Adaptation to Reality in Early Infancy. *Psychoanalytic Quarterly, 7,* 212-220.

Bennett, S. (1971). Infant-Caretaker Interactions. *American Academy of Child Psychiatry Journal, 10,* 321-335.

Bettelheim, B. (1976). *The Uses of Enchantment.* New York: Knopf.

Boss, M. (1963). *Psychoanalysis and Daseinanalysis.* New York: Basic Books.

Bowlby, J. (1969). *Attachment and Loss* (Vol. 1). New York: Basic Books.

Bowlby, J. (1973). *Attachment and Loss* (Vol. 2). New York: Basic Books.

Burlingham, D. and Freud A. (1942). *Young Children in War Time*. London: Allen and Unwin.

Cassirer, E. (1946). *Language and Myth*. New York and London: Harper.

Cassirer, E. (1953). *The Philosophy of Symbolic Forms* (2 vols.). New Haven: Yale University Press.

Deutsch, H. (1926). Psychology of Sport. *International Journal of Psycho-Analysis, 7*, 223-227.

Dunn, J. (1977). *Distress and Comfort*. Cambridge: Harvard University Press.

Edinger, E. F. (1972). *Ego and Archetype*. Baltimore: Penguin Books, 1973.

Eliade, M. (1958). *Patterns in Comparative Religion*. London: Sheed and Ward.

Ellenberger, H. F. (1970). *The Discovery of the Unconscious*. New York: Basic Books.

Erikson, E. (1950). Toys and Reasons. In *Childhood and Society*. New York: W. W. Norton, 1963.

Erikson, E. (1959). Identity and the Life Cycle. In *Psychological Issues* (Vol. 1). New York: International Universities Press.

Erikson, E. (1964). *Insight and Responsibility*. New York: W. W. Norton.

Erikson, E. (1968). *Identity, Youth, and Crisis*. New York: W. W. Norton.

Erikson, E. (1972). Play and Actuality. In M. Piers (Ed.), *Play and Development*. New York: W. W. Norton.

Erikson, E. (1977). *Toys and Reasons*. New York: W. W. Norton.

Fenichel, O. (1945). *The Psychoanalytic Theory of Neurosis*. New York: W. W. Norton.

Fordham, M. (1969). *Children as Individuals*. London: Hodder and Stroughton.

Fraiberg, S. (1977). *Every Child's Birthright: In Defense of Mothering*. New York: Basic Books.

Freud, A. (1946). *The Ego and the Mechanisms of Defense*. New York: International Universities Press.

Freud, A. (1965). *Normality and Pathology in Childhood*. New York: International Universities Press.

References

Freud, S. (1894a). *The Neuro Psychoses of Defence*. Standard Edition, 3. London: Hogarth Press, 1962.

Freud, S. (1894b). Obsessions and Phobias: Their Psychical Mechanism and Their Aetiology. *Standard Edition*, 3. London: Hogarth Press, 1962.

Freud, S. (1894c). On the Grounds for Detaching a Particular Syndrome from Neurasthenia Under the Description 'Anxiety Neurosis'. *Standard Edition*, 3. London: Hogarth Press, 1962.

Freud, S. (1900). The Interpretation of Dreams. *Standard Edition*, 4, 5. London: Hogarth Press, 1953.

Freud, S. (1905). Three Essays on the Theory of Sexuality. *Standard Edition*, 12. London: Hogarth Press, 1958.

Freud, S. (1907). Obsessive Actions and Religious Practices. *Standard Edition*, 9. London: Hogarth Press, 1959.

Freud, S. (1908a). Civilized Sexual Morality. *Standard Edition*, 9. London: Hogarth Press, 1959.

Freud, S. (1908b). Creative Writers and Day-Dreaming. *Standard Edition*, 9. London: Hogarth Press, 1959.

Freud, S. (1909a). A Case of Obsessional Neurosis. *Standard Edition*, 10. London: Hogarth Press, 1955.

Freud, S. (1909b). Five Lectures on Psychoanalysis (Second Lecture). *Standard Edition*, 11. London: Hogarth Press, 1957.

Freud, S. (1909c). Five Lectures on Psychoanalysis (Fifth Lecture). *Standard Edition*, 11. London: Hogarth Press, 1957.

Freud, S. (1910). Leonardo da Vinci and a Memory of His Childhood. *Standard Edition*, 11. London: Hogarth Press, 1957.

Freud, S. (1911). Formulations Regarding the Two Principles in Mental Functioning. *Standard Edition*, 12. London: Hogarth Press, 1958.

Freud, S. (1912a). A Note on the Unconscious in Psychoanalysis. *Standard Edition*, 12. London: Hogarth Press, 1958.

Freud, S. (1912b). Types of Onset of Neurosis. *Standard Edition*, 12. London: Hogarth Press, 1958.

Freud, S. (1913a). The Claims of Psycho-Analysis to Scientific Interest. *Standard Edition*, 13. London: Hogarth Press, 1953.

Freud, S. (1913b). Totem and Taboo. *Standard Edition*, 13. London: Hogarth Press, 1953.

Freud, S. (1914). On Narcissism: An Introduction. *Standard Edition*, 14. London: Hogarth Press, 1957.

Freud, S. (1915). Thoughts for the Times on War and Death. *Standard Edition*, 14. London: Hogarth Press, 1957.

Freud, S. (1917a). Introductory Lectures on Psycho-Analysis (Lecture XXII: Some Thoughts on Development and Regression—Aetiology). *Standard Edition*, 16. London: Hogarth Press, 1963.

Freud, S. (1917b). Introductory Lectures on Psycho-Analysis (Lecture XXIII: The Paths to the Formation of Symptoms). *Standard Edition*, 16. London: Hogarth Press, 1963.

Freud, S. (1917c). Mourning and Melancholia. *Standard Edition*, 14. London: Hogarth Press, 1957.

Freud, S. (1917d). Introductory Lectures on Psycho-Analysis (Lecture XXVIII: Analytic Therapy). *Standard Edition*, 16. London: Hogarth Press, 1963.

Freud, S. (1920). Beyond the Pleasure Principle. *Standard Edition*, 18. London: Hogarth Press, 1955.

Freud, S. (1923). The Ego and the Id. *Standard Edition*, 19. London: Hogarth Press, 1961.

Freud, S. (1924a). The Economic Problem of Masochism. *Standard Edition*, 19. London: Hogarth Press, 1961.

Freud, S. (1924b). A Short Account of Psycho-Analysis. *Standard Edition*, 19. London: Hogarth Press, 1961.

Freud, S. (1925). An Autobiographical Study. *Standard Edition*, 20. London: Hogarth Press, 1959.

Freud, S. (1926). *Inhibitions, Symptoms, and Anxiety*. Standard Edition, *20. London: Hogarth Press, 1959.*

Freud, S. (1927). The Future of an Illusion. *Standard Edition*, 21. London: Hogarth Press, 1961.

Freud, S. (1929). Civilization and Its Discontents. *Standard Edition*, 21. London: Hogarth Press, 1961.

Freud, S. (1932). Why War? *Standard Edition*, 22. London: Hogarth Press, 1964.

Freud, S. (1933a). New Introductory Lectures on Psycho-Analysis (Lecture XXXII: Anxiety and Instinctual Life). *Standard Edition*, 22. London: Hogarth Press, 1964.

Freud, S. (1933b). New Introductory Lectures on Psycho-Analysis (Lecture XXXI: The Dissection of the Psychical Personality). *Standard Edition*, 22. London: Hogarth Press, 1964.

Freud, S. (1940). An Outline of Psycho-Analysis. *Standard Edition*, 23. London: Hogarth Press, 1964.

Gadamer, H-G. (1972). *Truth and Method*. New York: Seabury, 1975.

Gertz, C. (1958). Religion as a Cultural System. In W. Lessa and E. Vogt (Eds.), *Reader in Comparative Religion*. New York: Harper and Row, 1965.

Greenacre, P. (1957). The Childhood of the Artist. *The Psychoanalytic Study of the Child, 12*, 47-72.

Greenacre, P. (1960). Considerations Regarding the Parent-Infant Relationship. *International Journal of Psycho-Analysis, 41*, 571-584.

Greenacre, P. (1971). *Emotional Growth* (2 vols.). New York: International Universities Press.

Greenson, R. (1965). The Working Alliance and the Transference Neurosis. *Psychoanalytic Quarterly, 34*, 155-181.

Guntrip, H. (1969). *Schizoid Phenomena, Object Relations, and the Self*. New York: International Universities Press.

Guntrip, H. (1971). *Psychoanalytic Theory, Therapy, and the Self*. New York: Basic Books.

Harlow, H. F. (1959). Love in Infant Monkeys. *Scientific American, 200*, 66-74.

Harlow, H. F. (1965). The Affectional Systems. In A. M. Schrier, H. F. Harlow, and F. Stollnitz (Eds.), *Behavior of Nonhuman Primates* (Vol. 2). New York: Academic Press.

Heimann, P. (1942). A Contribution to the Problem of Sublimation and Its Relation to Processes of Internalization. *International Journal of Psycho-Analysis, 23*, 8-17.

Hong, K. M. (1978). The Transitional Phenomena: A Theoretical Integration. *The Psychoanalytic Study of the Child, 33*, 47-79.

Horney, K. (1939). *New Ways in Psychoanalysis*. New York: Norton, 1963.

Jones, E. (1916). The Theory of Symbolism. *Papers on Psycho-Analysis* (Fifth edition). London, 1948.

Jung, C. G. *Symbols of Transformation*. Collected Works, 5. New York: Bollingen Foundation, 1956.

Jung, C. G. *Psychological Types*. Collected Works, 6. Princeton: Bollingen Foundation, 1971.

Jung, C. G. *Two Essays on Analytical Psychology*. Collected Works, 7. New York: Bollingen Foundation, 1953.

Jung, C. G. *The Structure and Dynamics of the Psyche*. Collected Works, 8. New York: Bollingen Foundation, 1960.

Jung, C. G. *The Archetypes and the Collective Unconscious*. Collected Works, 9(1). New York: Bollingen Foundation, 1959.

Jung, C. G. *Aion: Researches Into the Phenomenology of the Self*. Collected Works, 9(2). New York: Bollingen Foundation, 1959.

Jung, C. G. *Mysterium Coniunctionis*. Collected Works, 14. New York: Bollingen Foundation, 1963.

Jung, C. G. *Miscellany. Posthumous and Other Miscellaneous Works*. Collected Works, 18. New York: Bollingen Foundation, 1950.

Jung, C. G. (1961). *Memories, Dreams, Reflections*. New York: Pantheon Books.

Kalff, D. M. (1971). *Sandplay: Mirror of a Child's Psyche*. San Francisco: Browser Press.

Kasemann, E. (1965). The Righteousness of God in Paul. In *New Testament Questions of Today*. London: S.C.M. Press.

Kernberg, O. (1969). A Contribution to the Ego-Psychological Critique of the Kleinian School. *International Journal of Psycho-Analysis*, 50, 317-33.

Klaus, M. H. and Kennell, J. H. (1976). *Maternal-Infant Bonding*. Saint Louis: C. V. Mosley.

Klein, M. (1929a). Infantile Anxiety Situations Reflected in a Work of Art and in the Creative Impulse. In *Love, Guilt, and Reparation*. New York: Dell, 1977.

Klein, M. (1929b). Personification in the Play of Children. In *Love, Guilt, and Reparation*. New York: Dell, 1977.

References

Klein, M. (1930). The Importance of Symbol-Formation in the Development of the Ego. In *Love, Guilt, and Reparation*. New York: Dell, 1977.

Klein, M. (1932). *Psycho-Analysis of Children*. London: Hogarth Press, 1937.

Klein, M. (1937). Love, Guilt, and Reparation. In *Love, Guilt, and Reparation*. New York: Dell, 1977.

Klein, M. (1950). On the Criteria for the Termination of a Psycho-analysis. In *Envy and Gratitude*. New York: Dell, 1977.

Klein, M. (1952a). On Observing the Behavior of Young Infants. In *Envy and Gratitude*. New York: Dell, 1977.

Klein, M. (1952b). The Origins of Transference. In *Envy and Gratitude*. New York: Dell, 1977.

Klein, M. (1955). The Psycho-analytic Play Technique: Its History and Significance. In *Envy and Gratitude*. New York: Dell, 1977.

Klein, M. (1957). Envy and Gratitude. In *Envy and Gratitude*. New York: Dell, 1977.

Klein, M. (1958). On the Development of Mental Functioning. In *Envy and Gratitude*. New York: Dell, 1977.

Klein, M. (1959). Our Adult World and Its Roots in Infancy. In *Envy and Gratitude*. New York: Dell, 1977.

Klein, M. (1961). *Narrative of a Child Analysis*. London: Hogarth Press.

Kris, E. (1955). Neutralization and Sublimation: Observations on Young Children. *The Psychoanalytic Study of the Child, 10*, 30-46.

Langer, S. K. (1946). Translator's Preface. In E. Cassirer, *Language and Myth*. New York and London: Harper.

Langer, S. K. (1953). *Feeling and Form*. New York: Scribners.

Levy, D. M. (1937). Primary Affect Hunger. *American Journal of Psychiatry, 94* (2), 643-652.

Loewald, H. W. (1975). Psychoanalysis as an Art and the Fantasy Character of the Psychoanalytic Situation. *Journal of the American Psychoanalytic Association, 23*, 272-299.

Mahler, M. S. (1972). A Study of the Separation-Individuation Process. *The Psychoanalytic Study of the Child, 26*, 403-424.

Mahler, M. S. and Pine, F. (1975). *The Psychological Birth of the Human Infant. Symbiosis and Individuation.* New York: Basic Books.

Martyn, D. (1977). A Child and Adam: A Parable of the Two Ages. *Religion and Health,* 16 (4), 275-287.

May, R. (1961). *Symbolism in Religion and Literature.* New York: George Braziller.

Milner. M. (1952). Aspects of Symbolism in Comprehension of the Not-Self. *International Journal of Psycho-Analysis,* 33, 181-195.

Modell, A. H. (1968). *Object Love and Reality.* New York: International Universities Press.

Modell, A. H. (1976). "The Holding Environment" and the Therapeutic Action of Psychoanalysis. *Journal of the American Psychoanalytic Association,* 24, 285-307.

Murphy, L. B. (1972). Infants' Play and Cognitive Development. In M. Piers (Ed.), *Play and Development.* New York: W. W. Norton.

Neale, R. E. (1969). *In Praise of Play.* New York: Harper and Row.

Neumann, E. (1959). *Art and the Creative Unconscious.* New York: Pantheon (Bollingen Series).

Neumann, E. (1973). *The Child.* New York: G. P. Putnam's Sons.

Provence, S. and Ritvo, S. (1961). Effects of Deprivation on Institutionalized Infants. Disturbances in Development of Relationship to Inanimate Objects. *The Psychoanalytic Study of the Child,* 16, 189-205.

Racker, H. (1968). *Transference and Countertransference.* London: Hogarth Press.

Rey, H. A. (1941). *Curious George.* New York: Houghton-Mifflin.

Richardson, C. C. (1955). The Foundations of Christian Symbolism. In F. E. Johnson (Ed.), *Religious Symbolism.* New York: Harper (Distributor).

Ricoeur, P. (1970). *Freud and Philosophy.* New Haven: Yale University Press.

Ricoeur, P. (1974). *The Conflict of Interpretations.* Evanston: Northwestern University Press.

Ricoeur, P. (1976). Psychoanalysis and the Work of Art. In J. H. Smith (Ed.), *Psychiatry and the Humanities.* New Haven: Yale University Press.

Riess, A. (1978). The Mother's Eye: For Better and For Worse. *The Psychoanalytic Study of the Child, 33,* 381-408.

Roazen, P. (1975). *Freud and His Followers.* New York: Knopf.

Robertson, J. (1962). Mothering as an Influence on Early Development. The Psychoanalytic Study of the Child, 17, 245-264.

Robson, K. S. (1967). The Role of Eye-to-Eye Contact in Maternal-Infant Attachment. *Journal of Child Psychology and Psychiatry, 8,* 13-25.

Rodrigue, E. (1956). Notes on Symbolism. *International Journal of Psycho-Analysis, 37,* 147-157.

Rycroft, C. (1956). Symbolism and Its Relation to the Primary and Secondary Processes. *International Journal of Psycho-Analysis, 37,* 137-146.

Searles, H. F. (1965). *Collected Papers on Schizophrenia and Related Subjects.* New York: International Universities Press.

Sechehaye, M. A. (1951). *Symbolic Realization.* New York: International Universities Press.

Segal, H. (1952). A Psycho-Analytic Approach to Aesthetics. *International Journal of Psychoanalysis, 33,* 196-207.

Segal, H. (1964). *Introduction to the Work of Melanie Klein.* London: William Heinemann.

Spitz, R. A. (1958). On the Genesis of Superego Components. *The Psychoanalytic Study of the Child, 13,* 393-404.

Spitz, R. A. (1965). *The First Year of Life.* New York: International Universities Press.

Stern, D. N. (1971). A Micro-analysis of Mother-Infant Interaction. *American Academy of Child Psychiatry Journal, 10,* 501-517.

Stokes, A. (1973a). A Game That Must be Lost. In *A Game That Must be Lost.* Great Britain: Carcanet Press.

Stokes, A. (1973b). Psycho-Analytical Reflections on the Development of Ball Games, Particularly Cricket. In *A Game That Must be Lost.* Great Britain: Carcanet Press.

Stokes, A. (1973c). On Resignation. In *A Game That Must be Lost.* Great Britain: Carcanet Press.

Sullivan, H. S. (1953). *The Interpersonal Theory of Psychiatry.* New York: W. W. Norton.

Sullivan, H. S. (1965). *Personal Psychopathology.* New York: W. W. Norton.

Tillich, P. (1948). *The Shaking of the Foundations.* New York: Scribners.

Tillich, P. (1955). Theology and Symbolism. In F. E. Johnson (Ed.), *Religious Symbolism.* New York: Harper (Distributor).

Tillich, P. (1961). The Religious Symbol. In R. May (Ed.), *Symbolism in Religion and Literature.* New York: George Braziller.

Tillich, P. (1963). *The Boundaries of Our Being.* London: Collins.

Trible, P. (1978). *God and the Rhetoric of Sexuality.* Philadelphia: Fortress Press.

Ulanov, A. and B. (1975). *Religion and the Unconscious.* Philadelphia: Westminster Press.

Ulanov, B. (1977). *Sublimation and the Boundaries of Self.* Anglican Theological Conference. Austin, Texas.

Van der Leeuw, G. (1963). *Sacred and Profane Beauty.* New York and Nashville: Abingdon.

Von Franz, M. L. (1970). *An Introduction to the Psychology of Fairy Tales.* Zurich: Spring Publications, 1973.

Walder, Robert (1932). The Psychoanalytic Theory of Play. *The Psychoanalytic Quarterly,* 2, 208-224.

Wickes, F. G. (1927). *The Inner World of Childhood.* New York: Mentor, 1968.

Winnicott, D. W. (1947). Hate in the Countertransference. In *Through Paediatrics to Psycho-Analysis.* New York: Basic Books, 1975.

Winnicott, D. W. (1950). Aggression in Relation to Emotional Development. In *Through Paediatrics to Psycho-Analysis.* New York: Basic Books, 1975.

Winnicott, D. W. (1954). The Depressive Position in Normal Development. In *Through Paediatrics to Psycho-Analysis.* New York: Basic Books, 1975.

Winnicott, D. W. (1958). Psycho-Analysis and the Sense of Guilt. In *Maturational Processes and the Facilitating Environment.* New York: International Universities Press, 1965.

References

Winnicott, D. W. (1960). The Theory of the Parent-Infant Relationship. In *Maturational Processes and the Facilitating Environment*. New York: International Universities Press, 1965.

Winnicott, D. W. (1962). A Personal View of the Kleinian Contribution. In *Maturational Processes and the Facilitating Environment*. New York: International Universities Press, 1965.

Winnicott, D. W. (1971). *Playing and Reality*. New York: Basic Books .

www.ingramcontent.com/pod-product-compliance
Ingram Content Group UK Ltd.
Pitfield, Milton Keynes, MK11 3LW, UK
UKHW041417180426
11947UKWH00007B/180